Sindhi Journeys of Faith

Sindhi Journeys of Faith

Deepak & Celia Mahtani
with
Sindhi Friends

Second Printing - August 2011

Cover design by Megan Snelgrove

Published by Deepak and Celia Mahtani

Printed in Hong Kong by:

China Alliance Press
Website : www.cap.org.hk

ISBN 978-0-9569821-0-0

Contents

Dedication

We dedicate this book to:

- our ancestors and parents who brought us out of the Sindh and endured hardship and heartache to rebuild their lives outside their homeland. We salute them and dedicate this book to their memory and to their sacrificial giving.
- our awesome God who has given us new life, new hope and a guarantee of eternal life in Him beyond the grave.
- our children, Arun and Sanjay, to whom we leave this legacy behind.
- our 'adopted' children Pooja and Manesh, who have accepted us into their lives.
- to all Sindhis around the world who would enter into our journeys.

A book written
by Sindhis
about Sindhis
for Sindhis
around the world.

We thank Tom, Barbara and Serenity Ward for being part of the editorial team. We also thank those who contributed their stories and all those who have helped, prayed and encouraged us along the way.

Introduction

The Sindhi people are well known for their rich culture, strong work ethic and close family ties. Most people associate Sindhis with being successful businessmen and women as business seems to run in their blood. Empires created by the Chanrai, Chotirmal, Dalamal, Doulatram, Harilela, Hinduja, Lokumal, Melwani and Shivdasani families to name just a few, are renowned the world over. However, Sindhis are also prominent in the arts and media, publishing, law, education and politics. Today, there are Sindhis in every country from Afghanistan to Zimbabwe. This is a brief attempt at compiling stories of Sindhis around the world who have come from the Sindh, journeyed across the globe and gained much success not only in social, education, material and financial terms but also in terms of their own spiritual journeys. We have tried to include a cross-section of ages, professions, geographies, situations and genders to ensure as much of a balance as possible.

When requested, we have not used actual names, to protect individuals and their families. However, these are real stories of real people in real situations. They include people you may know with surnames such as Advani, Boolchand, Chugani, Dadlani, Melwani, Nanwani, Panjwani, Sakhrani, Tolani, Vaswani and Wadhwani.

Our hope and desire is that you may be encouraged by these stories. Each one, by sharing their story, has made themselves vulnerable. However, they have done so to share with you some of their most intimate experiences which you might be able to associate with and see yourself reflected in them. The common strand though them all is these Sindhis who came from Hindu, Sikh, Muslim and no religious backgrounds have, in their journeys of life, encountered the God of the Bible, of which our great Mahatma Gandhi himself said,

"You Christians look after a document containing enough dynamite to blow all civilisation to pieces, turn the world upside down, and bring peace to a battle-torn planet."

We hope and pray you will read these stories with an open mind and an open heart. Our desire is not to coerce, convince or convert anyone. It is only for God to reveal himself to each person. We personally know each one whose story is included in this book, which is why we have referred to them as 'friends'. We know that none of these individuals have been forced to convert - they chose to follow Jesus by choice. This book is simply our attempt to say to you in humility and love, "this is my story — maybe one day it could be yours as well."

Our belief is that faith is not an event, it is a journey and our prayer is that along your journey, you will meet with the God who loves you as you turn the pages and meet our friends...

One of the greatest emperors who ever lived, Napoleon, who many Sindhis respect more than many other leaders, once said of Jesus,

"Alexander, Caesar, Charlemagne and I myself have founded great empires; but upon what did these creations of our genius depend? Upon force. Jesus alone founded His empire upon love, and to this very day millions will die for Him.

"I think I understand something of human nature; and I tell you, all these were men, and I am a man: none else is like Him; Jesus Christ was more than a man...I have inspired multitudes with such an enthusiastic devotion that they would have died for me ... but to do this it was necessary that I should be visibly present with the electric influence of my looks, my words, of my voice. When I saw men and spoke to them, I lighted up the flame of self-devotion in their hearts...Christ alone has succeeded in so raising the mind of man toward the unseen, that it becomes insensible to the barriers of time and space.

"Across a chasm of eighteen hundred years, Jesus Christ makes a demand which is beyond all others difficult to satisfy: He asks for that which a philosopher may often seek in vain at the hands of his friends, or a father of his children, or a bride of her spouse, or a man of his brother. He asks for the human heart; He will have it entirely to Himself. He demands it unconditionally; and forthwith His demand is granted. Wonderful!

"In defiance of time and space, the soul of man, with all its powers and faculties, becomes an annexation to the empire of Christ. All who sincerely

believe in Him, experience that remarkable, supernatural love toward Him. This phenomenon is unaccountable; it is altogether beyond the scope of man's creative powers. Time, the great destroyer, is powerless to extinguish this sacred flame; time can neither exhaust its strength nor put a limit to its range. This is it, which strikes me most; I have often thought of it. This it is which proves to me quite convincingly the Divinity of Jesus Christ."

Emperor Napoleon Bonaparte

Moving from Darkness into Light

Deepak Mahtani
Management Consultant in the UK

My mother and father were both born in India. They left their hometown shortly after partition in 1948 and went to Bombay for a few years where my two oldest siblings were born, and then they moved from Indonesia to Singapore to Hong Kong where I was born (the youngest of five children) and finally to Japan where I lived for 14 years. While we had financial challenges, my father was fairly successful in business. I moved to Switzerland at the age of 18 for university studies and then set up the European office for the business. I lived in Geneva for 14 years and then came to the UK with my wife Celia and two sons.

My parents were Hindus and my mother and two sisters were very religious. They went to pujas and satsangs and had people like Hari Om Sharan to stay in our house. We men did the minimum to keep the peace at home. My father was too busy with the business and that, combined with the 'success' orientated society of Japan, drilled in the fact that success was the way to be happy and fulfilled in life. Thus started my career and I was determined to achieve success at any cost. I worked ten hours a day, seven days a week, with no holidays. By the time I was 25, I had everything I had possibly hoped for: a nice income, a flashy car and a comfortable apartment. I was travelling around the world, living in 5 star hotels and dining in some of the best restaurants. In many ways, life was very good and I did not have time to think about religion or spirituality.

Despite all this, I felt an emptiness within myself that could not be filled. I had always thought that happiness could be found in money and possessions. The more you had the happier you were. Money could buy anything: happiness, pleasure and the good things in life. But I found that this was not so. The more I had, the more I felt that something was missing.

I could not understand this. Aristotle Onassis, one of the richest men in the world, said at the end of his life, *"I finally got to the top only to realise that there was nothing there."* A wise Chinese millionaire told me a few years ago: *"Even travellers cheques aren't accepted in heaven. We can take nothing with us from this world when our days are over."*

Then a tragedy occurred in 1984. My sister, who was 28, died in a car accident while visiting me in Geneva. The phone call from the police that morning was devastating. I was very close to her and her death caused me to ask many questions: Why do bad things happen to good people? What happens after death? Where has she gone? What is the purpose of life? Is there a God out there somewhere? What would happen if that happened to me? That was November 1984. I became extremely angry with the world and people and stopped seeing anyone. I was depressed and could not sleep at night.

I needed to find answers to my questions and decided to go through the teachings of the major religions of the world. I started with the Hindu scriptures since I was from a Hindu background. Then I read the Koran, the Bible and teachings of some of the gurus and philosophers of Buddhism. Nothing I read seemed to give me any answers and I became more confused. I wanted to know with certainty where I had come from, what I was doing here and where I was going to go when I died.

In the spring of 1985, I met a Sindhi friend who I had not seen for three years. As I began to tell him what I had gone through, the tears poured out. I asked him my questions. He told me where he found his answers in his own search for truth some years earlier and how he became a Christian. He suggested I read the Bible again and invited me to the church he attended.

Being an Indian, a Sindhi and a Hindu, the very thought that the Christian faith could possibly have the answers was frightening. *"East is east and west is west and never the twain should meet."* Everything that I associated with my idea of the Church was negative: dark, cold buildings, the pompous Pope, old fashioned songs, a Western religion. What troubled me now was how this Sindhi friend could be a Christian and even be happy about it.

I started reading the Bible again and over several months things started to make sense. I remember I would ask the same questions again and again of different people just to make sure their answers agreed. I also started attending a Young Adults Group and made some new friends. One of the young women in this group was also a Sindhi and although I did not know it then, she would one day be my wife (but that's another story). Who says marriages are not made in heaven?

From my study of the Bible I came to the following conclusions about God, myself and my relationship with him. I realised that God was the God who created the world and that included me. He showed me that he is a loving God who cares for me. He is also a holy God and cannot accept any kind of wrongdoing. Even though I had not killed, stolen or been a bad person, I realised that in God's eyes my pride, my anger and my selfishness were wrong and did not please God. God's penalty for this was a separation from him and a lack of peace. However, God wanted to restore my relationship with him. He sent his son Jesus Christ to earth to die on the cross to pay the penalty on my behalf. Jesus, a man without sin died the most horrible death possible and was willing to do so. Why? Because He loved me. This was a staggering thought! I did not have to do anything but ask for God's forgiveness and accept his offer. If I accepted Jesus as my Saviour and Lord, God would accept me and I would have a right relationship with him.

It was then that I realised that my previous impressions of the God of the Bible were wrong. This God is not a Western God. He is not a God only for the Americans or the English but for every race, colour and language. Jesus Christ is not a blond haired, blue eyed, white faced English gentleman in a pin striped suit. If anything, being of Middle Eastern origin, his appearance was closer to our own Asian look: brown skinned, with dark hair and eyes and wearing sandals and robes.

In April 1986, my office staff sent me on a holiday, because they thought I needed to get away and were afraid I would do something to harm myself. I went to Tenerife. It was Easter Sunday and the warm sun was bright. I often heard the church bells ringing, but this time they sounded different. In them was a voice saying, "Come to me," and I thought of Ernest Hemingway's book For Whom the Bell Tolls. I felt the bells were Jesus calling me to come to him. I finally fell to my knees beside my bed and decided to accept God's offer of life and asked Jesus Christ into my life to fill the void that was still there. But I made a condition with God. I said, "I accept you but I have not needed you in the past. If you break a single promise to me you can go out in the same way you came in." This was such an arrogant prayer for me to pray to the Almighty God, but the amazing thing is that He accepted even this prayer.

Since then there has been no turning back. My relationship with God is right. I know what will happen to me after I die and I no longer live in fear each and every day. The void has been replaced by peace. But, becoming a follower of Christ is not an insurance policy against hardship, disease or death.

I suffer from a hereditary kidney disease that took the life of my mother and two uncles. I used to ask my father why I lost my mother when I was only 12 and he said it was her karma which I found hard to accept. Then in 1991, I was diagnosed with the same disease that took her life. There was much suffering and hardship as a result. I tried to accept this as best as I could and settled for a less than totally normal life. My faith in God helped me cope.

On March 10, 1995, I went on the British kidney transplant waiting list being told I would need to wait for at least two years due to my blood type. I started dialysis on March 14th and ten days later on March 25, I received a call at one in the morning from the hospital advising me that they had a kidney for me. Against all odds of blood type and a waiting list of 5000 people, God provided in a most miraculous way. It is a new lease of life that God has given me and I realise I am living on borrowed time. I am truly thankful to God for a new physical and spiritual life.

Reflecting back on my life, if I were to review the first half compared to the last half, I can see that I was living in darkness. But it is only once I was exposed to the light that I could actually see how dark it really was and how much more there was to life. Until then, the darkness was my reality and the realm in which I lived. If you have been in a dark room or place for an extended period of time, your eyes adjust to the darkness and you function. It is like the life of a blind man. If you were to ask a blind man what it was like to live life, he would say that he walks, breaths, thinks and eats just like any other person who can see. That is his reality and he does all things from that perspective.

Part of my work now involves charity work and I am involved in a hospital project in North India. Last October I was in one of the hospitals where they have cataract operations for the blind. I spoke to one old man who was born blind. He had three grandchildren whom he touched, held and talked to but had never seen - he never saw the smiles on their faces. He described them vividly even though he was blind. I met him again the day after his operation and for the first time he could see the smiles on their faces. You should have seen his face - his reality of darkness was transformed having received his sight - light instead of darkness.

How much of our lives are lived in the reality of living in the dark - not having seen the pure light that God offers? A blind man was asked, *"Is there anything worse than being blind?"* He thought for a moment and replied, *"What is worse is being able to see and choosing not to."*

After my sister died, my father disappeared, leaving his business and cutting all contact with any of us. He went to the mountains of India to live a life of a hermit to find peace. After three years he returned still not having found any meaning to his life. He remained in darkness and doubt. I once read a story about a man in a desert who woke up hungry in the middle of the night. He lit a candle and began eating dates from a bowl beside his bed. He took a bite from one end and saw a worm in it, so he threw it out of the tent. He bit into the second, found another worm, and threw it away also. He thought that if he continued he would not have any dates to eat so he blew out the candle and quickly ate all the dates. I could identify with this story, as for many years I preferred darkness and denial instead of facing the reality of the emptiness of my life and needing the light.

If I share my story with you today, it is not because I have all the answers. But rather I come to you as a beggar who was hungry for the bread of life, telling you where I found it and where you also can find it. You could have a similar story. In my search for truth, what made the God of the Bible different from the other gods were two things:

1. The Christian faith is the only one in which God reaches down to man. All other faiths are man's attempts to reach up to God. God SO loved the world that he gave his only Son, Jesus Christ

2. The God of the Bible is not a God promoting a religion but rather a God who wants a relationship with you and me - a very intimate daily one.

God so loved the world but more importantly, HE LOVES YOU and ME. In fact the Bible is not a religious book but rather a love story: Ye pyar ki kahani hai. He is a personal God who I can speak to at any time and call, Papa, Baba or Abba. He is my Father, my Brother and my Friend.

This is the God I do not have to try to please with offerings or gifts - no pujas and no artis are needed. This is not a God whom I have to fear will strike me down if I do something wrong. My life and all that I do are no longer controlled by fear but by love. He is a God who is the creator, the sustainer and the protector. He is a personal God with whom I can communicate directly without having to go through any holy priest, a God to whom I have direct access through his Son Jesus Christ.

Can You Have Chicken Makanwala with Christ?

High School Teacher and Homemaker in Hong Kong

From an early age, I was taught to love the various Hindu gods with an open heart and I did. I would join my mother in her daily worship and during her monthly Sat Narain Kata felt incredibly holy as the waves of incense floated around me. My sister and I would quarrel over whose turn it was to bathe the miniature statues in milk or adorn them with our hand-made ponchos and blood red 'thilk'. I was also taught that the gods rewarded good deeds and obedience. So everyday I would ask the gods for my heart's desires. I believed that I rightfully deserved to receive whatever I prayed for - after all I was vegetarian every Monday wasn't I?

During my university days, I was never into drinking, smoking or swearing. I was simple, I was drawn to simple people and in my second year at University, most of my friends happened to be Christians. They were friendly and I had fun with them although I was sure I would never be one of them. Yet, over time, I saw something in them that seemed to make them wiser, with a quiet confidence, even when life was difficult. This made me curious about the source of their wisdom and confidence.

My 20th birthday fell on a Sunday and I asked my friends if I could tag along with them to Church, just to see what all the fuss was about. The first timeI heard Christian worship, I felt like laughing and crying all at the same time. The words were beautiful, people sang from the depths of their hearts with their arms reaching out in praise and I felt a presence that I had not known before. I have to admit that I felt a little awkward singing the name of Jesus at first as I was not used to it, but through the music I learnt about Him - and then I met Him and He humbled me.

It hit me that Jesus, the son of God, did not come on a chariot or with a bow and arrow, like some of the Indians gods I had grown to know. He did not defeat his enemies by shooting them down. He was not adorned with jewels or seated on a royal throne like many of the gods I had heard about. He came with one sole purpose, as a servant king to reconcile you and me with God the Father through being the ultimate sacrifice. He came to die for us. He came knowing he would be rejected and beaten and that his bones would be broken. This God seemed more real to me than any other god I had prayed to in the past.

Soon after this experience, a friend of mine gave me a Bible with a short guided study on the book of John. This study went from being a 5-minute browse to a 30-minute daily period of transformation. Reading about the life of Jesus moved me in a way I had never known. I wanted to love like Him, to show compassion, patience and generosity in the same way. It was like the words in the Bible came alive and spoke directly to my heart. Then things would happen in the day, situations where I would otherwise be jealous, malicious or unforgiving and words from scripture would leap up into my head from the night before and I would choose to act differently. I would choose to follow Jesus and the most amazing things would happen, leaving me bursting with joy.

This faith was not about my self-gratification. Nor was it about earning my way into blessing because Jesus loves us as we are. More than that, it was not about being fearful of God but instead, of entering into a loving relationship with a father, brother and friend who I could talk to everyday because He had suffered in every possible way on this earth so He always understood. It made so much sense.

Over time, my faith grew. But also over time my fears grew too. I wanted my life to change from being self-centred to God-centred, but I felt alone - and I was angry with God. Why had He revealed Himself to me, only so I would have to worship Him alone? Where would I ever find a life partner who understood God's grace and majesty and still craved chicken makanwala for dinner? I decided that I would never find anyone who would truly understand my faith. It was better to forget the God I had found, so I returned home and put my Bible away in the toilet cupboard...

After a year or so of not having God in my life I realized I needed Him more than ever. I once again had trouble forgiving people and dealing with guilt myself. I knew that Jesus could set me free from all this as in Him I always had the strength to forgive and He always took away my baggage of guilt, so I decided to pray for help. A few nights later, I was having dinner with a friend who was telling me about this Sindhi guy she had met the weekend before. He was great looking and intelligent, but there was one major drawback. He was... a Christian! Could this be my makanwala man I thought? And guess what? He liked biryani too!

When I was ten years old, I was a brownie guide and took part in the annual sports day at Stanley Fort. I remember being very excited because I had been paired up with a petite ginger-haired girl for the three-legged race and whenever we practiced together, we would just fall into a perfectly synchronised step so we ran like the wind and I knew I was going home with a gold rosette that day! When we arrived and I was warming up before the race my partner was nowhere in sight. I started to panic. I couldn't run this race, not without her. With two minutes to go, she showed up and I beamed. We carefully tied our inside legs together, as if to permanently fuse them, and stood ready. At the sound of the gun we flew, but a few steps into the race down she fell. I scooped her up and off we were again when suddenly I lost balance and tripped. As the ground came closer to my face I squeezed my eyes shut preparing for the pain but was yanked up before I could hit the ground. She held my back and I held hers and knowing that, it was not long before we reached the finish line and won the race!

Now that, to me, is a wonderful picture of marriage. I did not want to marry unless the man I married and I were of the same mind. When I married my husband, it was as if our hearts were fused together with God's seal, never to be separated. As we ran, when I fell he would be quick to forgive me, to stay running with God and to pick me up. When he fell I would be quick to forgive him, to stay running with God and to pick him up. So we were always destined to win the race, right?

Well, we did not really know how fast each of us ran until our hearts were fused. So after marriage I discovered that my husband runs a lot faster than me. He gets by with less sleep than Jack Bauer and he drives like he is James Bond! It also turns out that sometimes when he falls, I am angry and do not want to pick him up by forgiving him because I feel wronged and hurt. So in the process of holding onto my pride and pain, I fall down too.

Now how are we going to win the race of life if we're both down on the ground eating mud? And the truth is we both do it. We are both easily offended. When you think about it, it is foolish,each sitting and sulking on the 'running field' during a 'race'. Not only that, sometimes we are even tempted to temporarily untie the handkerchief that 'binds our legs'. By that I mean sometimes we let the sun go down on our anger without reconciling our differences or go for days without speaking to each other, going completely against God's command. So we each go off in separate directions for a run around the field but again how is that going to help us win the race? We just waste time and energy. It is tempting at times, when you are angry to think, "I don't need him, I can run faster without him and win this race on my own." But the truth is, even if I reach the finish line first, I will not win anything, I will just be disqualified.

Over the years I have come to refer to the Bible

as the best guide for married couples. In Ephesians, husbands are commanded to love their wives as Christ loves the Church. Christ loved the Church so much that He led us, covered us, served us and even died for us. My husband has to love me that much? Sounds good to me! What does not sound so appealing is that as a wife I am commanded to submit to my husband, as the Church submits to Christ. I have to acknowledge and respect that he is the spiritual head of our household. This is easy to do in theory but it becomes challenging when my husband makes decisions that I do not agree with. It is also hard to submit on days when he does not quite seem like he would die for me, but God does not say submit when he loves you, He just asks me to submit. I continue to struggle with this, but I have learnt that God is sovereign and when we trust and obey Him in faith, we are always blessed with His best for us.

Larry Crabb said that many of us stand at the altar and silently repeat the vow, "I give myself to you for the rest of my life for you to meet all of my needs." Naively we think that if we marry, all our needs will be met. To make things worse, when I married my husband, a whole bucketful of the highest expectations came with me. Surely my husband would always be ready to forgive, have total understanding, be unendingly patient, anticipate my every need and the list goes on. And over the last nine years, I have discovered that my husband cannot meet all my needs. Actually, he is not supposed to be able to because there are three of us in this marriage, my husband, myself and God.

In Ecclesiastes 4:12, it says, *"Though one may be overpowered, two can defend themselves. A cord of three strands is not quickly broken."* What I am learning everyday is that our husbands cannot fully satisfy our needs. They can provide feelings of love and acceptance but our sense of self-worth can only be founded on the unconditional love that God alone can give. None of us are perfect so we must go to the perfect one to be filled. What I have learnt is that until I am aware that my needs are already met in Christ, I am motivated by emptiness to meet my needs. When I am free from self-centred preoccupation of my own needs then it is possible to give to others, especially to my husband. I can only give out of my fullness, when I am empty I have nothing to give.

I was drawn to Jesus because He came to serve, not to be served. It was never about His gain or His pleasure. If I want to follow Him, I believe the best training is in marriage. If I choose to make God part of this marriage everyday and first look to Him by taking time to be filled by His word and submitting first to His Holy Spirit, then my needs will be met and I will be full to give my best to my husband and family. Our first command is to love the Lord our God with all our heart, mind and soul and then to love our neighbour as ourselves. My husband is my closest neighbour. My first ministry as a believer is to him!

Mike Mason said, *"In marriage a man will cleave to the woman and the woman to him - the way his own flesh cleaves to his own bones. Just so does the Lord desire to invade our deepest privacy binding us with Him our whole lives long and even into eternity with cords of blood."* It is a beautiful picture and my prayer is to grow old with my husband, to be bound together in God's grace and mercy, and over time, to fall into perfect step with my soul mate as we one day cross that finish line together and meet our Saviour face to face.

Finding a Friend at Virginia Tech

Dinesh Bhojwani
Businessman in USA

I was born in the summer of 1969 in the city of Secunderabad which is in the state of Andhra Pradesh in India. My parents had migrated from Sindh (now in Pakistan) during the time of the partition of India in 1947. After the partition, they lived in Ajmer (Rajasthan) for a while and then made their way to Secunderabad mainly following business prospects. Life in Secunderabad was a lot of fun for me because I was surrounded by many cousins of similar age and had many friends in Lal Bahadur Nagar, a middle class neighbourhood.

I still remember the various festivals that we celebrated as a neighbourhood, which for us kids was like one big family. Even at home, being the youngest of three boys, I enjoyed a whole lot of love and attention. A fond memory I treasure is how we celebrated my ninth birthday. My mom and I hired an auto-rickshaw, rode it to the local vegetable market, loaded it with various vegetables and fruits and headed to a nearby orphanage. At the orphanage, my mother laboured with the resident cooks to prepare a feast for everyone, and I got to serve! Wow! What a blessing to have a family that taught us to serve at an early age!

When I was 11, my father moved to Dubai for better prospects. During the next 4 years, we travelled to Dubai every year for 3 months, and he would visit us for a couple of months. This went on until I finished the eighth grade and then the rest of us moved to Dubai as well. I remember life in Dubai being an upscale version of that in India, with many amenities and recreational activities. I was making a new set of friends in high school and getting acquainted with a new culture at the same time. After a few years, all of a sudden my father became very sick and died of cancer within a few months. His death shook my 15-year-old perfect world for the first time and it never was the same again. After his death, my brothers worked hard growing the business that he had started, to give me the opportunity to study abroad. I started preparing to go to the United States for higher education.

I went to Blacksburg, Virginia as a freshman at Virginia Tech in 1986 when I was only 17. It was very scary to begin with, not knowing what to expect. Pretty soon, I got involved in a fraternity as it was my firm desire to make lots of friends, not knowing that this would lead me to a path filled with alcohol, which I enjoyed at the time. At the end of my freshman year, I was booked to go back to Dubai for the summer. On the last day of exams, after my math exam, I stumbled upon a poster on the billboard about a summer job in California.

Something in me made me call the telephone number on that ad, and later in the day I showed up for a meeting where a bunch of Tech students had signed up to go to California to sell books door to door. By the next day, I was in a convoy of 14 cars on my way to California for the summer. While in California, I met Nick, a fellow student from Tech. Each morning, Nick would be out of the apartment before any of us woke up. He said that he was seeing a friend, and I was curious as to what he was up to. I found out that the friend that he was talking about was Jesus Christ, which puzzled me as I had never heard of Jesus before, let alone in the context as a friend!

Summer passed by, most of us saved a little bit of money after paying all the bills, made lifelong friends, and learned that sales was hard work! I returned to my life as a fraternity brother and life went on. However, later in the year, I got sick a few times due to excessive drinking and all of a sudden I got a strong feeling that I would die soon if I continued on this path. This made me read a lot about various world religions. I started with the Bhagwad Gita (the Hindu scriptures), the Quran, Zen Buddhism, Taoism and other such material.

Hinduism taught me about the circle of life, rebirth, and karma. I knew that even if I had many births, there is no way I (or anyone else) could live a sinless life. Buddhism taught me that one has to be without sin to achieve Nirvana, and the only way to do that was to remove desire from our life, as desire is what leads to sin. At that point, the only way to remove desire from a young man would be to end his life. That would not work! The more I read, the more I thought that I was doomed! I remember reading the Five Pillars of Islam and thinking that no one I knew followed these completely. Similarly, Taoism taught me about compassion, moderation and humility, which apart from being great virtues cannot lead to a sinless life or cleanse one of the sins already committed.

My sophomore year ended and I had decided to live off-campus so had to find an apartment soon. Then one day, I saw Nick on the drill field. He was also looking for an apartment! We became roommates the following year and Nick gave me a Bible to add to my collection of religious books. After looking at it on the shelf for some time, I eventually picked it up and started reading the Bible. I started with the book of John. While reading about Jesus, His claims and His teachings, I needed a lot of help as I could not understand any of His parables.

That is when I started meeting Nick to help me study the Bible. After reading about Christ and His claims, I could see a difference between all the other books I had read and the Bible. The other books were mainly a to-do list, but the Bible was about God loving us no matter what, and showing that love to us by sending His only son to die for us in our place on the cross! Jesus said, *"I am the way, the truth and the life. No one can come to the Father except through me."* Those were bold claims that I read! In those days, Nick read me a verse from the Bible - *"for I know the plan I have for you, plans to prosper you and not to harm you... If you seek me with all your heart, you will find me, says the Lord."* I wrote this on a piece of paper and stuck it on the wall next to my bed, and would read it every night and ask God to reveal himself. A few months later, there were a series of mornings when I awoke in a cold sweat. After a couple of these occurrences, I called my American host mom, Mrs. Randall, to come to see me. And that is when with her help I gave my life to Christ by acknowledging the fact that I was a sinner and by asking Jesus to forgive my sins and thanking Him for dying on the cross in my place. (The Bible says in Romans 10:9 that if you confess with your mouth that Jesus is Lord and believe in your heart that God raised Him from the dead, then you will be saved.)

All I can tell you is that in the months to follow, I felt a burden lifted. I was beginning to understand the meaning of having Jesus as your best friend, a living God, who gave up His own life for me so that I can be united with Him (if I choose Him) for ever! How awesome! The Bible says that we all have sinned and fallen short of God's glory, and that the wages of sin are death and separation from God forever. It also says that Jesus died for us so that we may live with Him forever. That is possible if we open the door of our heart and invite Him as our Lord and Saviour. All it takes is to confess your sin and have faith in Him.

I thank God for bringing a whole set of new friends into my life shortly after I put my faith in Him. I started attending the Fellowship of Christian Athletes at the campus of Virginia Tech in Blacksburg, Virginia with Nick, where I was soon surrounded by a group of new friends who were very hungry for God's word. This started my adventure in really getting to know my creator - how He created this world, anointed a group of people to be His people, how those people turned their back on Him and how He eventually sent His own son to be sacrificed for the sake of all our sins!

I remember visiting various churches and noticed how each one had its own unique style of worshipping God! Early on, the good Lord blew me away with a radical answer to a need - at the start of a new college semester, my roommate Jay Cash was without cash and needed to pay for his meal plan in order to survive the semester. This burdened me very much as I loved Jay. I gave this to the Lord in prayer on the following Sunday when the Pastor invited anyone with a need to come up to the pulpit and pray. After pouring my heart out in front of God and the church congregation whom I had never met before, each one got up from their chair that day and made a love offering towards Jay's meal plan! What an awesome God!

A couple of years after I became a follower of Jesus, I graduated from Virginia Tech with a Bachelors in Electrical Engineering in 1991 and returned to Dubai to be reunited with my family, except that this time I had my best friend,Jesus Christ, with me. This led to some of the most testing times in my life, during which I faced my family and tried to convince them that my belief in Jesus was a part of my rescue operation by God, and not some white man brainwashing a gullible Indian student.

As time passed, I met the second love in my life, Ritu, who with the challenging past of a dysfunctional home, had moved to Dubai from Delhi. Today, I see His fingerprints on how I met Ritu, her expressing hopelessness in life and embracing Jesus when she got to know Him. Soon our love story started, which resulted in us getting married in Dubai in 1995. Soon after that, her siblings became followers of Jesus as well. The years after our wedding were a combination of blessings and trials.

We attended a non-denominational church in Dubai where we were encouraged and discipled by many including the current Youth pastor, Peter Dale, his wife Ruth, elder Frank Raj and his wife Christine.

A few years later in 1999, the travel bug hit us, and we moved to the US (Blacksburg, Virginia) with our firstborn, Nishant, who had just turned one. With this began my second phase in Blacksburg, this time as a married entrepreneur. Soon after we moved to Blacksburg,where Roshni and Rishi were later born, the Lord showed us His plan by introducing Steve Edwards who had a strong desire to reach out to Indian students at the campus of Virginia Tech. This led to the formation of the Indian Christian Fellowship, a gathering of Indian students interested in knowing the God of the Bible and the plan of salvation through Jesus Christ. Over the years, as we met weekly in our home for praise, worship and Bible discussion, we saw the Lord bring many students from different backgrounds. These uncles and aunts (as our kids addressed them) blessed us weekly with their desire to know God. What a joy it was to watch the change in these young men after they opened the door of their hearts to let Jesus in!

I have been a follower of Jesus since August 1989, when I invited Him into my heart. In these past twenty years, I have experienced many peaks and valleys, during which His promise - *"I will never leave you nor forsake you"* - has been a real comfort. I know that He has begun good work in me, which hurts at times.

When a sculptor starts working on a piece of wood, He has the plan of the end result in His mind.

If the piece of wood could feel every strike of the chisel, it would scream. Similarly, when the Master uses His chisel to mould me into 'the plans that He has for me', it hurts. At those times, trusting Him (which is difficult) has brought about a joy which surpasses my understanding.

I am not sure if you have ever invited Jesus into your heart. If you have, then you know that God has always loved you and has an awesome plan for you. And if you have not, I know that He is standing at your heart's door and knocking (trying to get your attention).

Will you let Him in?

An Ordinary Person Meets an Extraordinary God

Kamla Sadhwani
Housewife in the Philippines

My name is Kamla Sadhwani. I am an ordinary person from an ordinary family. My parents are both of Indian origin and are Sindhis. My father died when I was ten years old and my mother had to care for ten children. Life was hard. My eldest brother had to leave school even while my father was living to help in the family business. My eldest sister also had to leave school to help out. I, being younger along with my other brothers and sisters, had the opportunity to finish high school and get some college education.

My parents were both Hindus, however since we were in the Philippines, the better schools were the Catholic Schools, and therefore we had our education under Nuns and Priests. We were taught the Catechism as part of the curriculum and therefore became Catholic. There was also a ruling at that time that all students be baptized before being accepted at that school. My parents were not strict Hindus, so it did not bother them that we went to church on Sundays and joined in whatever Christian activities were required of us.

I had reached the age of 18 when my mother suggested a match for me in marriage. I felt I was cheated out of my youth, especially because I had three sisters who were older than me and at that time were not yet married. In our culture, it always puzzled me that the boys had the right to choose and we girls just had to obey the decision of our parents. At that time, it was my mom and my eldest brother who made the decision.

At first, I did not want to be married so I ran away with a boy pretending that I would marry him. He wanted to help me and he thought that I would stay with him and eventually get married to him, but I had a different plan. I told him that I wanted to see a priest and when we went to the convent, I told my story to the priest and he arranged for me to stay with the nuns until I decided what to do.

In the meantime, my fiancé started to look for me and regardless of what he had heard, he still wanted to marry me. My mother was devastated with what was going on, and I could not bear her tears as she begged me to go through with the wedding. In obedience, I agreed.

Once married, my life changed dramatically. I had the opportunity to travel and then I had children, four in all. My husband, having a typical Indian culture, ruled the house. He came and went as he pleased and had lots of friends who drank and gambled. Marriage was hard for me. This was not exactly how I expected my married life to be. I felt empty even when I used to go to church every Sunday.

The hunger for something I did not understand was growing deeper in my soul. I was lonely and sad most of the time and I felt there was no joy in living. There was no meaning to anything that was happening. As I started searching, I learned about some Gurus who were in town to give lectures.

I longed to hear what these Gurus had to say about what life was all about, because I knew this was not it. There was something missing.

Swami Chinmayada was my favorite lecturer. He was extremely intelligent and everything he said made sense until we had an opportunity to speak to him one on one. I asked him one question, "What happens to us when we die?" His answer to me took me back to where I had come from, totally dissatisfied and even disgusted. He said that when we die, it is like waking up from a bad dream. He said that this world is all an illusion and when we die we will just merge with the Almighty and be one with him, just like a drop of water that falls into the sea. We will lose our identity and cease to exist. Of course, this is also after several life cycles.

I could not accept this, perhaps because of my Christian training when I was younger. It raised many questions adding to my confused state of mind. I decided to continue going to Mass every Sunday hoping that one day I would be able to understand what life was all about. Going to Mass was a discipline I had learned from Catholicism. It did not change who I was and it still felt that I was left in the dark to solve all my problems on my own. I had no one.

One day my nephew, Raj Kumar Mirpuri, invited me to go with him to the World Christian Fellowship. It was already known at that time that they were Protestants and we as Catholics were told not to attend their services so I was skeptical about joining him but he kept inviting me. Perhaps the Lord knew that I was looking for Him and He sent someone to help me. I finally decided to go and attend a service. I could not believe what I heard. Relationship with Jesus Christ! Who had heard such a thing? I was curious and continued to attend the service every week, but I also never stopped going to Mass every Sunday. It took two years to convince myself that I did not need to go to Mass. One Sunday, I received the Lord and I knew then that I was never going to be alone.

I am now involved with the Fil-Indian Fellowship Church here in the Philippines. We are now about 35 full members and we average 70 church goers on a Sunday. My troubles and struggles continue even now, but I am not lonely and alone anymore. The Lord has worked in my life since then. I am maturing everyday as I learn more and more about the Love of Our Lord Jesus Christ and Our Father in heaven.

Readers, I challenge you now. If you feel that nothing has happened in your life, come to Jesus, and He will show you the meaning of life and will never leave you alone.

Changing Religion or a Changed Life?

Balu Dadlani
Businessman in Hong Kong

My name is Balu Dadlani. I was born in Mumbai, India. I am from a Sindhi family and I have been living in Hong Kong since 1985 with my wife and three children. Though one could say I am from a Hindu background, my family did not actually perform any of the Hindu rituals. In fact we never had any statues or pictures in our house and never went to a temple or performed pujas, because my family followed a Guru who taught about the brotherhood of man and peaceful, harmonious living with others, irrespective of their faith or belief.

When I was growing up I was not very interested in faith or religion. Sometimes, when I would go with my mother to satsangs, I would understand the vichar (message) of the guru, which was basically about living in harmony, not becoming too materialistic and so on, and most gurus in India have similar teachings. Many of them quote from different holy books like the Gita, the Ramayana, the Koran or the Bible.

The guru we used to follow discouraged idol worship believing that God has no form and is everywhere including in each of us. Therefore, at the satsang, we used to touch the feet of each other to take a blessing since we considered that God is in each one of us. In fact, one thing that always stuck in my mind was that there would be a rush and queues would form to touch the guru's feet. At that time I wondered why people were queuing because I considered the guru 'human' too, just like the next person so why the queue to touch his feet?

I used to hear comments like, "we were so close to him (the Guru), we had such good darshan (worship) of him." I would think in my mind, "But he is just human like you and me," although I never expressed these thoughts aloud. It was also very common to wash the Guru's feet with water and then take that water and treat it as holy water. We used to drink it when we were sick or during exams and so on. Though I was not really a keen follower of that Guru and my mind was open to every religion, I used to think there is one God but different ways of reaching him.

When in India, I was involved in bad company and did many things that would not be appropriate to mention here – but I hope the words "bad company" convey the message to you. I moved to Hong Kong when I was 18 and struggled a lot for the next 20 years. I worked for others for a couple of years and then started my own business but during those 20 years I never progressed very far financially – it was just survival.

When I came to Hong Kong I was single and alone and had much more freedom than in India so some of my wrong habits continued. I had my family's religious background and, although they had the same satsang in Hong Kong, I did not go there even once. I was not serious about faith but I did like to discuss and argue about it. I guess it was mostly to have a conversation and I was trying to impress people. I used to read a lot and listen to different messages from different gurus.

When I was in my mid-twenties I met my wife-to-be and we dated for some time. She was from a Catholic background and some time later we decided to get married. I was so open to different faiths and religions that we decided we would have a church wedding as well as a wedding in the temple, because I respected all religions.

In fact I was against people converting just because of marriage. I had a Hindu friend who married a Catholic girl and she agreed to become Hindu. She actually started doing pujas and so on. I accepted that people sometimes change their religion because they have found a true God in that other religion, but I just could not understand how somebody who had followed one religion all her life could just change in one day not because they felt the religion made more sense to them but because their husband was of that religion.

After we got married, my wife continued to go to the Catholic Church. Sometimes I accompanied her but I used to find it very much like a ritual, no different from the Hindu faith or guru background that I had come from. There was no real meaning, no growth and no change of life. It was just something you did because of tradition or because you were born into a Catholic or Muslim or Hindu family. You never understood or questioned your faith or beliefs; you just followed all your life and then passed it on to your children and so on.

I somehow could not follow that. In fact I feel most religions are like that. If you really question people and ask them about their faith, they do not know much about what they believe in. I used to discuss this with my wife and she told me that she felt that way too. But she also told me she had met some other friends and she found them different. She felt they were getting something out of their faith, it was not just a ritual they were doing or a tradition they were following. She told me of her desire to go to such a church and soon she found one near our house and started going there. She began to notice that there really was a difference between the church that she had been going to and this new one.

To me it did not make any difference, this church or that church, as long as she was happy because although I generally had a lot to say or discuss, I was not truly in search of God at that time. I believe today that unless you are truly seeking and searching for God with your heart you will not come to know him. You could be stuck in rituals or charity or gurus, but if you truly want to know God, you have to desperately seek the truth.

Sometime later, my wife told me about a program which had some catchy title, "What is life" or "Change your life" or something like that. The title attracted me and as my wife was out of town, I decided to go alone to that event. While I was there I heard a guy from South Africa tell a big audience about how he had come from such a bad background. He had taken drugs and sold them, he had been in prison and he tried to kill himself more than once. Then he said that it was because he came to know the true and living God, Jesu, that he was alive that day and standing there. What surprised me at the time was how this guy was willing to tell the audience all about his dirty past. I felt that there must be something, some power that made this man do so much for what he believed in. Towards the end of the program there was an announcement asking those who needed prayer to indicate this and I too asked to be prayed for. That night as I was going home, I felt very relaxed, like some big burden had been taken away from me. I felt good. I surely felt different.

A few days later we received another invitation to an evening party and this time my wife came along too. During the middle of the program a guy came on to the stage and started telling everybody about how he had been cheating on his wife and had had several affairs. He and his wife had many fights and they had almost split up because of his behaviour. His wife was sitting just a few rows ahead of us. I was surprised how he could have such courage to admit his past faults, mistakes and wrongdoings not only in front of a big audience but also in front of his wife. Later he came down from the stage and he and his wife hugged each other and they had tears in their eyes.

Then another man went up on the stage. I remember he had hurt his leg badly because he had a crutch and had to be helped on to the stage. I remember I thought this guy must be really desperate to come here even with a broken leg. His story was also similar. What stunned and surprised me through all this was that there was something going on. I had never seen people come on stage and humiliate themselves in front of the public just so that they could tell you about their new life or changed life. This created a desire in me to find out what the secret of a changed life was and I started truly seeking for knowledge of God. As I sought Him, He revealed himself to me and I found him in the person of Jesus Christ, the Son of God.

I know many people think that today I am a Christian because my wife is from that background, but if they only knew the kind of proud man I was that would be impossible. All along the way, when I was considering following Christ I used to think the same thing, "What will people say?" or, "People will say I changed my religion for my wife." But somewhere along the way I thought, "I have a choice — I can continue thinking about what people will think or say, or, I can have a relationship with God."

I am glad to tell you that I chose to know and pursue God and it was the best decision I have ever made. My prayer and desire would be if you too could seek and find Him. This is the truth. Look at the three guys I mentioned I saw on stage and look at my story and the others in this book. Why are we doing this — these are not just stories – they are changed lives.

Has anybody from your faith, religion or belief come and told you about their changed life? I do not know about you, but with all the friends and relatives I have, I have never had anybody come and tell me.

Friends, all I can tell you is that you too, like many others, could be stuck in traditions or rituals or do religious things that you have no idea about or the reasons why, or, you can come to know

God. You may have a lot of questions and doubts but if you truly seek you will find the truth. Jesus himself said, *"Seek and you will find."*

God's Faithfulness to Me and My Family

Housewife in Indonesia

Born in a very strict Hindu family, I was the 8th of 11 children. I was very religious and a seeker of God from a tender age. I pondered about death many times. Having heard of reincarnation, I would wonder what would happen to me after my death? What about my family? The thought of death and separation would make me very depressed and so I tried to live a righteous life so that I would somehow escape suffering and live happily.

From a very young age I became a worshipper. We had a small temple at home where statues and pictures of deities were kept and every morning I would bathe and clothe the gods, put flowers on each statue, burn incense and sing songs of worship. In the evening I would put the gods to sleep by singing lullaby worship songs and with deep reverence bow before them. This I did, thinking that my sins were being washed away and that I was becoming purer, holier and more pleasing to God every day.

I would visit my cousins and at times stay in their homes. My younger cousin and I would perform the same rituals morning and night: burn incense and sing worship songs. One day, after finishing my rituals, the same cousin, looked at the statues and pictures of the deities and told me bluntly that these are not gods, but devils! She told me that Jesus is the true God and that one day He is coming back to take His people home, all those who believe in Him. Of course I was shocked — how could anyone say such a horrible thing! But surprisingly I did not ask too many questions and immediately believed in Jesus.

The thought of Jesus coming back to take me to heaven, made me so happy, that I would pray, "Make it soon." Some of my cousins had given their hearts to Jesus through the witness of their Chinese neighbours and so they shared the good news with us. My two sisters, one of my brothers and I became Christians initially and later on others followed. We were given an old King James Version Bible with small print which was very difficult to understand but because we were so hungry for God we would read this Bible daily.

We began to read from the beginning, in Genesis, and continued to pray fervently. We could not keep the good news to ourselves so we shared it with our families, friends and neighbours. At first my mother thought we were just children and in due time we would forget all about it. But when the family saw that we had stopped going to temples and refused to worship their gods, they became very angry with us. Severe punishment from our family and the Indian community followed and my mother could not take this. Almost every day she would cry, scream and beat her chest and head. At times she refused to eat, threatening to commit suicide and actually attempting it many times. Persistently, she would tell us to return to Hinduism, the religion of our family and our culture.

Forty years ago, changing one's religion was

unthinkable. It was considered a serious crime, very shameful and humiliating to the family. The Indian community ostracized us. They threatened to put us behind bars. Once we were called by the police who questioned us about our faith. Parents warned their children against us.

In the temples, the elders made an announcement to keep their children from being friends with us. They even started a special school to teach their children about Hinduism and train them to read their holy books. There was so much fear in the community, that the elders would have meetings to discuss how to stop Christianity from spreading because many Hindus were being converted to Christ. We were forbidden to attend church, or to visit our friends and cousins. We were not even allowed to make phone calls. We would read the Bible and pray secretly in the toilet. This treatment and punishment increased day by day. The atmosphere at home became very tense. There was much crying and mourning.

It was very depressing at times especially when we were of the age to be married. No Christian guys were available at that time and my mother and some elderly relatives would come and give us long lectures pressurizing us to marry unbelievers. At times it was so overwhelming that I was tempted to run away from home. Mentally I was exhausted. The thought of waking up every morning became so great a burden that I wished I could sleep endlessly because I could not handle the atmosphere. But amidst all these terrifying moments, we never stopped fasting and praying.

Occasionally we met a missionary lady from Bandung, who would encourage us and pray for us. In fact it was she who gave us reading materials, such as books of revivalists like Jonathan Edward, Charles G Finney, Charles and John Wesley, Oswald J Smith and Andrew Murray. I was so inspired by these books that zeal and fire rose up within me. Then I asked God to take away my sleep so I could pray unceasingly for the whole world to be saved. The thought of the lost going to hell was so horrifying, that I began to have passion for lost souls. My constant cry to God was to send revival.

My mother would go to India for long periods and these were the times I would talk to God for many hours. I didn't care if there was rain or sunshine. I became very intimate in my relationship with Jesus. At times I would feel Him so close like He was holding my hands and walking with me and I would be filled with such unspeakable joy that I would sing love songs to Him with adoration and intense devotion. Suddenly I would hear myself singing as if Jesus was responding to my love for Him. The book of Songs of Solomon became my favourite book and I found myself so deeply in love with Jesus that I would call Jesus my husband and my lover. It was at such intimate moments that God's love would overwhelm me like a blanket. He would assure me through the Holy Spirit again and again that He would give me souls. The sign that He gave me was that one of my sisters, who was a follower of philosophical teachings and was considered a leader by the people, would come to the Lord.

It was many years later I realized that a ministry was being birthed out of my intimacy with Jesus. Several years later, even though persecution was still on, I felt the Lord telling me to start going to church. I did and I was surprised to see people I had been praying for, even though we were not allowed to meet. God's timing was perfect and as soon as I started attending the church with my sisters and brother, the Lord impressed upon my heart to start a fellowship and the name was given from the Bible. We started this fellowship in 1986. It grew and grew. Truly, after six months, the sign that God had given me about my sister came to pass. She gave her heart to the Lord and now she is a pastor! No longer is she a philosophical teacher but a teacher of the good news. Now there are at least three Indian churches including ours and many Sindhis also attend other churches in our city. God kept His word as He did to Abraham. 'I will multiply you and make you a great nation.' I am expecting a great revival and have not stopped praying for lost souls.

Now what about my mother? One day she became so sick that she almost died so she called all her family and relatives together. Two doctors came to see her. Her blood pressure had reached its peak! It was during that time she pointed a finger at us saying that we would be responsible for her death. So she, along with others, insisted that we give up our faith for her sake. It was one of the greatest trials we had to face. In spite of all those angry looks directed at us, we did not give up, even for a moment. The Holy Spirit reminded us about the power of God, through the stories in the Bible.

Even though we had not yet started attending church, we were called merciless and heartless. We were greatly criticized but God is great. He never allows His children to be defeated. My mother was healed and lived another 35 years! Three years before she died, she gave her heart to Jesus and at night she would call out the name of Jesus shouting Halleluiah! We saw a lot of miracles. God never left us, just as He promised. 'I will never leave you nor forsake you. Lo I'm with you, even to the end of the age.' At times He removed the storm but many times He walked with us through the storms.

At present we are distributing tracts to apartments and putting them in malls and in whatever way we can we are still spreading the gospel. We believe God's word shall never return void but shall bring forth fruits for His glory. When I look back and recall all that I have been through, I wonder what it was that held my faith and kept me going. I realise it was nothing but the Word of God and communing with the Lord!

Hallelujah!

Glory to God!

Surprised by the Hand of God

Michael Vashulal P Massand
Real Estate Broker in New York

"You will see me and find me when you seek me with all your heart. I will be found by you," declares the Lord. Jeremiah 29:13-14

One of my earliest memories goes back to August 20th,1947, during the India/Pakistan partition. At the age of seven years, I was in Quetta during the Marshall Law curfew and saw the whole city burning. My mother, two sisters, sister-in-law and brother were trying to take refuge in the next door neighbor's house by crawling through the small passageway that joined the houses roof to roof. My oldest brother was away on a business trip and I was the youngest of two sisters and three brothers. We lost everything because we were Hindu Sindhis who happened to live on the Pakistani side instead of the Indian side. We had to leave our home and everything in it and came to the city of Indore as refugees in India, with nothing. God blessed my family in Indore, where we lived comfortably in a bungalow and owned a car and I was educated in a Co-ed convent school from the first grade through to the end of high school.

In 1951, I was in the fifth grade and had a dear friend named Haikon. Whether he was Chinese or Korean I am not sure, since in those days we did not note any differences of race, color or creed. We were best friends. One day, he told me that he was not going to come to my home ever again. I asked him for the reason several times, but he kept saying that he was not going to come. Truly, he never came to my house again because right after that day, his dead body was found floating in the river. It was the saddest day of my young life thus far.

When I was 13 years of age, my mother was diagnosed with cancer. She suffered terribly and finally she died. It seemed that a heavy storm of sorrow and responsibility came upon me. Right after my mother's death, I almost died with a fever of 106°F. I wished for death, but God had different plans for me. My father and my oldest brother had a fight and our family was split. My pregnant sister who had been married for just one year returned home for good. Her in-laws had almost killed her. My parents had no choice but to bring her back. Prior to my mother's death, she asked me to make sure that I would not leave my sister alone but live with her always. So I moved in with my sister, and with her meager income we barely made it. With much struggle, I completed high school at the age of 17, and found a job in a Government office with a minimum salary. I worked days and went to college in the evening.

While in college, I had a Sindhi best friend, Chandru. Even though my sister and I were struggling to support ourselves and her young daughter, I had a fantastic time all around at work and at college. My social life was great. My best friend and his family were like my own family. One day my friend became very stubborn and told his parents that he wanted to go to Bombay for good.

While he was gone, I became stubborn as well and asked my sister to send me also to Bombay, not permanently, but for few days. After keeping a fast for 15 days, I won her consent.

I arrived by train in Bombay on Diwali,1960, in the early morning at 6 a.m. and stayed at my aunt's home in Dadar, a suburb of Bombay. I was so excited; I could not wait to leave all my gear at my aunt's place and go to see my friend in Chambur, another suburb of Bombay. I arrived at his place around 9:30 a.m. and knocked at the door to ask for him, but his aunt said he had just left for Bombay and would return in the evening. I left him a message that I was in town, feeling sure that he would come to see me in Dadar. To my surprise and concern, he never came. So the next day, I went again to Chambur to see him. This time when his aunt opened the door, her voice resonated with a deep sadness, "He is dead." She told me that the day before, when Chandru left for Bombay by train, he was hit by an electric pole on the head and was gone in two hours because of the internal bleeding in the brain.

That was a great shock, too much for me to bear. I went crazy. I became a philosopher searching for the meaning of life. It seemed that life was like a dream. I could not catch up with the past and rationalized that there was really no present. We really live with the past and future. Ah! Life is long but unpredictable. Did I ever know that I would have to go through all these sad parts of my life or that I would lose my loved ones? They were all gone and I could not even do anything to make them stay with me. It was a deep mystery that man is living, walking, talking, eating, thinking and doing but yet he has no control over his life. Where did he come from? Where does man go after he dies?

I questioned everyone I met from young to old, from pundit to scholars and philosophers, and I read many books. I wanted to find out where my friend went after he died. No one could answer. I decided to die, and find out where I was going (during that time I could not think logically that I would not know where I was going after death if I was already dead). That night I took a whole bottle of pain reliever pills before sleeping, assuming that I would not wake up in the morning. To my surprise, I woke up normally but very confused, not understanding why I was not dead.

Well, I did not give up and wrote a letter to my sister about my attempted suicide. Two days later, I took my bike and rode to a big lake in Indore which was about 7 miles across. When I walked out on the pier toward the center of the lake, there were two fishermen there. This was very unusual, since no one ever fished there. The fishermen were not moving or looking, but sitting there like statues. I was waiting for them to leave so that I could jump. While I was waiting for them to leave, my heart became very heavily burdened and I heard a voice say to me, *"Go back, you will see places and you will meet people."* It was so powerful that I had to go back.

I could not kill myself. I did not know what to do and was very frustrated. All my family, relatives and friends were concerned about my welfare, never leaving me alone.

Three months after my attempted suicide, I got an airplane ticket to go to Hong Kong from my new employer, who hired me without seeing or interviewing me for the job. Everyone insisted that I must go and encouraged me in every way possible. I did not want to go and leave India because of my sister and my job with All India Radio Station. I loved my job and I loved India.

I knew I would not get a passport, because in those days, one had to have immovable property (Real Estate) in order to get a passport. Somehow, looking back it seems like God Himself poured His favor, love and grace upon me. I got the passport without any difficulties. My sister insisted that I must go. I arrived in Hong Kong in March,1962. My quest of finding the truth about life and God was not over. Whoever I met, I always asked them about life. Somehow, I knew in my heart that I would find the answer.

Strangely, I studied in Convent school where Christian fathers and sisters (nuns) were our teachers and they spoke to us about Christ almost every day. I was the first one to reject Jesus Christ and I even rebelled against the school. Even though I heard the beautiful and heartfelt story of Jesus Christ in the third grade, I would not accept Him because of our patriotic family's strong faith in Guru Nanak. In our family line were the treasurers of Guru Gobind Singh (Sikhism) in Sindh. We were members of Congress during the revolution against the British. In spite of all that glamour and fame of my family, I don't think I had any faith or belief in anything. I had lost my faith when I lost my loved ones. I was hurting in my heart and I had an obsession to find the truth about man's life and destiny.

I did not give up my quest for 13 years, and during that time many people came into my life who gave me the gospel of Jesus Christ. What had He to do with me, I reasoned, since I was a Hindu and an Indian? God put me in a Hindu family and I belonged to my family. How could I believe in Jesus, the God of America, Europe and Australia, when we had our own gods? How could I abandon my family, my culture, my religion and my nation for Jesus or the gospel? There were many struggles in my heart, mind and soul and between heaven and the world.

I did not recognize the truth because my eyes, mind and heart were closed and I was blinded. There were a few people who had so much patience with me, and they walked with me for two years telling me about Jesus. They never got upset but always loved me and accepted me.

One day, March 21,1973, at 2:30 a.m., I was very upset, angry and frustrated and felt I could not take the world any more. Out of my anger I called on Jesus saying, *"Jesus, if you are truly the Son of God as people say, you come into my heart and life right now, and if you do not come now, I will never believe you."* Oh! My Lord Jesus! My Lord Jesus came in my heart instantly and filled me completely I started weeping bitterly. I could not remain upright but fell to the floor for several hours. I knew that the Lord poured Himself upon me. My whole life was running in front of my eyes as a movie. He revealed to me that He had been with me all my life and was waiting for me to come to Him.

The Lord Himself had spared my life from those pills I took to kill myself, and those two men sitting at the lake were not men but His angels. The voice I heard in my heart saying, *"Go back, you will see places and meet people,"* was His voice. I was crying bitterly. It was Jesus who came and poured out His mercy upon me. I came to know how much He loved me and how much He wanted to have a relationship with me and speak to me. I felt so ashamed before the Lord for what I had done to reject Him. I cried nonstop. My eyes, ears, mind, heart and soul were open. I felt myself like a dust particle before the Lord. I was convicted of being proud, boastful and prejudiced against everyone, even God Himself. My heart was full of penance. I was crying out very loud with confession of all my sins and shortcomings.

Instantly, I felt beautiful with eternal peace in my heart. He satisfied all my questions on religion, society, family, life and death. I felt that I was standing in front of the creator of the whole Universe, the Heaven and the Earth. What is religion, social structure, race, color or creed before Him; He is the creator of all. He only made man, not all those things which man has created. I realized that it is man who is trying to gain the world but is losing his soul.

The Lord transformed me spiritually inside out, and I felt like I was in Heaven. I found the Almighty God Himself and my heart was completely full of contentment, peace, joy and happiness. I started praising and worshipping Him. I prayed like I never prayed before. It was awesome and beyond understanding and explanation. I felt His presence in my heart, mind, soul and body.

Since that moment, 37 years have passed by, and I still feel His presence in my heart, mind and soul. I know I have eternal life and that I am going to heaven when I die. My quest is satisfied! AMEN!
Hallelujah!

The Father I Never Knew

Homemaker in Nigeria

It was March 6th, 1994, 3 a.m. in the morning, when the divine connection was made in my life. I sat on my bed, defeated and tired of life. Having had enough of the struggles I was facing, I had decided to end it once and for all. I had collected about 120 pills of Valium (sleeping pills) and had made arrangements not to be disturbed in the morning to give no opportunity for being revived. I lay reading the book Death of a Guru about a man who had lost his father who was a guru looked up to by thousands. Having lost his Father, he was appointed the next guru by tradition and had thousands looking up to him for assistance though he knew nothing and felt none of the powers that his disciples claimed he had. This caused the young man to go in search of the true God that his subjects were seeking in him. He found Christ but I had not yet reached that part of the book when suddenly I felt like I had 20 hands, all closing over my throat. The strangling sensation was so real, (I was so sure that there would be marks if I looked for them) the place suddenly felt eerie, fear gripped me and in the struggle, all I did was scream 'Father'.

Now this was not the done thing. I had never addressed anyone in my life as Father, and in the Hindu/Sindhi religious background that I grew up in, the term Father was not used. It was a surprise to me; I was calling someone who I did not know even existed. But He knew me. I heard a voice say,

"I love you," and immediately the hands left me. It was as if He had made a claim on me.

Fear disappeared and even as I sensed that this was real, I responded to the voice. *"But nobody loves me, and I do not like my life."* I heard from Him again, *"I will change your life for you."* I responded again, very boldly this time, *"But I will not compromise."* The voice spoke again to reassure me, *"I will not let you compromise.'"* I felt at peace, hugged my pillow and wept myself to sleep, not with pain or sadness but with a comfort that someone loved me and would take care of me.

I woke up the next morning, unaware of the changes that had happened or of the new life I had just received. My cook, Catherine, who had been with me for almost five years and who knew me better than anybody else, came up to me and asked me if she could pray for me. She had never done this before. Catherine led me in prayer and I made Jesus my Lord and my Saviour and invited the Holy Spirit into my life. I still did not recognize Him for who He was, and what He was doing with me. I just knew that somebody had taken over but little did I realise that this was a relationship I was getting into with the Father I never knew.

I was the only surviving child of my parents. My mother had had four children previously, but two had miscarried and the other two had died of leukaemia. My parents wanted to abort me rather than suffer leukaemia again, but God intervened. I was born with no illness and hospital visits brought my parents the joy that it was over, that they had been blessed with a daughter who did not have the disease.

My parents shared a beautiful relationship that they cherished so much, which did not give place to anything but love and respect for each other. They stood up for each other, understood and helped one another, never spoke in loud voices and cared deeply for each other. Sadly, my marriage was not like that. My husband was a wonderful man, a kind, god-fearing, good human being who would not even hurt a fly but we were arguing and fighting every day. We pretended to be the best couple in public but were totally apart at home, even staying in different rooms. Finally, one day, the whole thing exploded. My husband decided to let his family know as now he wanted to be set free from this marriage of pretence.

I tried everything I could to make my marriage work, even visiting a guru regularly. He blamed first one thing then another and suggested different prayers and pujas with every visit but nothing worked, and all hope for my marriage was gone. Then I met the Father I never knew.

I started praying every day with my cook because I did not know how to pray. I had been taught to recite prayers in my religion, but Catherine talked to God as though she was with someone. I was used to prayer being just a lot of space, a feeling of a lot of distance, not even sure of being heard, forget about being answered! Now I knew that I was being heard, that this God who is the Father I never knew cared for me and was always at work sorting things out for me. My nanny also presented me with a Bible; I started reading it and it was as if God was talking to me. He always comforted me, encouraged me and strengthened me. Within a week I had given up gambling and alcohol, which were my means of drowning my sorrows. My friends thought I had gone crazy. I refused to go to any religious gatherings and that offended my family. My Father started showing me many things and helped me exercise the power He had given me in Christ Jesus.

I had actually known my husband since I was a baby. His parents and mine were good friends. In fact it was his mother who had stopped my mom from aborting me. She had four sons and wanted a daughter so she pleaded with my mom to carry on with the pregnancy, that the child would be a daughter and that she would take care of her. Well, that is what happened; I came and did grow up in her house as her daughter. She passed away, and many years later, I became her daughter in-law.

There is a custom in Hinduism that calls for all sisters to tie a 'raakhee' on the wrists of their brothers confirming the covenant of their relationship in which the brother commits to taking care of his sister for life. Being an only child, and having these four boys around me, I used to tie 'raakhees' on all four of them, thereby making the covenant of brother and sister. This was now creating a problem. We could not be husband and wife. My Father showed me that it is He who makes these relationships and we have no right in going about making brothers, sisters or mothers of people. I had to repent and nullify all those covenants I had made. My father in-law was also married twice, having the second wife while the first was still alive. He had been separated from the first one for many years until the second one passed away with cancer. This was a generational curse and that had to be broken too.

Every day, my Father would show me things and how to tackle them. I had not yet started going to church but was helped by some Christian friends to understand the Bible. The Lord taught me many things, especially how to love. I loved my husband so much now in spite of the fact that he had not actually changed, but that is what my Father taught me, to love unconditionally and sacrificially. My husband started to drift more, having being told that it was not his fault but the gods, the births and the wrong connection with me. My father in-law arrived from India and strangely I found myself telling him not to condemn my husband but to support him because everybody had blamed him. My father-in-law agreed with a promise from me that I was surely coming back to the family. I left with him for India only to return within six months having received even more from my Father.

My Father performed many signs through me while I was in India. It was difficult for family and friends there to accept me as a Christian but as I spoke with boldness of my Father and all that He is and can do, I actually found them asking me to pray for healing and people were healed. This was new and very exciting for me too. I had read about it but was now experiencing it.

One beautiful experience I had was when there was no electricity and, being the rainy season, there were lots of mosquitoes. It was just impossible to sleep. It was 10 p.m. and everyone had already retired to their rooms when the lights went out. I took it up in prayer and lo and behold, the lights were back on in five minutes. My fan worked, my repellent worked and I went off to sleep. I woke up to my parents' voices at my door who were shocked to see that there was electricity in my room. Apparently the lights were not yet back on and it was not only our house, but the whole street that was affected. The fridge and freezer had totally defrosted yet the fan and repellent were working in my room. As soon as I woke up, they stopped too. I had sweet sleep that night, thanks to my Father who I never knew but was getting to know so much about.

Eventually my parents accompanied me to church and I told them of all the things that my Father was telling me. I also visited my father-in-law, encouraging him and telling him of all the promises God had made to me of restoration in my marriage. He loved to hear this as the topmost priority for him was to see his son's marriage blessed. During one of these visits, my mom gave herself to Christ. She just told him that she loved Him, thanked Him for saving me from suicide and decided to give up everything for Him in spite of being well known and very well respected by her guru. She used to organise everything when her guru came into town. She motivated people to believe but now here she was, giving up her faith and her guru to believe in Christ. This was a very big step but she was bold. She took down the huge portrait that hung in her living room and threw it out as though something had just struck her and she was not wasting any time.

Her coming to Christ was now taking us to another series of events. It was a matter of shame that a faithful and true disciple like her had left. The guru himself was interested and sent his chief disciple to come and talk to her. That day was exciting. It is a custom to fall at a guru's feet but my mom only welcomed him with a lot of love. She started praising the recent changes in her life. Her heart had been transformed. She, who had never even done anything for the maid at home, was now welcoming vendors and feeding them. She had given up gambling, which she could not do in the past. She had a peace that she had never experienced before, not even at their religious gatherings. The guru's disciple tried to argue about Christ but eventually had to leave seeing how strong she was and how much she loved God.

My mom had an amazing walk with God. Nothing interested her but to speak to the Father, hear from Him and do things for Him. Now my mom only knew how to read and write Sindhi, which is a language spoken in Pakistan, a Muslim country. She would sit each day on the balcony with an old radio station that was transmitted from Pakistan. She heard sermons, praised, worshipped and prayed - all in Sindhi. How awesome is our Father, ministry in Sindhi from a Muslim country - just amazing! She grew in Him, was strengthened and stood up for Him. She started hearing from her friends now, not because they wanted to talk to her but because they wanted to taunt her about what God had done to her daughter. They had heard about me, but my mom told them that I was there only for a short while, that what they had heard was not true and that I was going back soon.

My mom continued to grow in her faith, I would say she was stronger than me; she helped, encouraged and prayed for those who came to her. She lived six years longer and died very peacefully. She was laughing and talking to my dad when she just closed her eyes and was gone. My dad was shocked; he had never seen anyone go in this manner. My dad also accepted my Father as his, and Jesus Christ as his Lord and Saviour. I am very grateful for I know that they are both in heaven and I will see them when I get there. This is a promise from my Father and I no longer struggle to do good works to make it there but am led by His Holy Spirit to joyfully do the works that please Him.

Three months went by; my Father was teaching me to love. He helped me to forgive my husband, love him and accept him for who he was. I noticed with my Daddy that He did not want anything to have a hold on me. I was not going to love only if I got love, I was not going to give up masturbation only if my husband pleased me, I was not going to forgive only if someone apologised and made it up to me and I was not going to be good only if someone was going to be good to me, but I was going to do all these by His power and love that was flowing through me so that no matter what the circumstances I would not lose my joy or peace and always be found in the place of victory.

One night I woke up and had a vision. It was not a dream because I was awake. I realised that I did not have my little finger on my right hand.

I immediately asked, “Father, where’s my little finger?” By now He was so real and near to me that I conversed with Him as if He was right there with me. He asked me if I was willing to give up my finger for my husband. I immediately agreed. I was willing to give up all my fingers. I do not know why that happened but I instantly had all my fingers back and the next day my husband called and said that he was coming to fetch me back. I guess God just wanted to know if I was ready, full of love and really willing to do anything for him. My Daddy’s priority is Love. Everything is done in Love. Love has to be the background, the setting, the atmosphere and the attitude. He cannot operate without Love; He is Love. He is not bound by circumstances or attitudes or desires; He just loves.

My meeting with my husband was not what I had imagined, being swept up in his arms with angels fluttering around over us. In fact it was painful. He just called and asked me to come over, not even coming to visit. No one in my family wanted me to go like that, but my parents were so confident of my Father in heaven that they let me go. They trusted my Father to take care of me more than they could. That night was miserable, and I cried like I had never cried. My husband was distant, making polite conversation, and that was horrifying. I did not know what I was getting into. The next day was Christmas and I left for church, where I cried even more and came back still feeling empty. My husband was waiting for me and just hugged me from behind, making sweet promises to me, apologising for what he had done coming so late to pick me up, giving me all his reasons and also telling me I was the best and that he was going to treat me like a queen. Wow, the angels were not fluttering but I sure was. My Daddy is great!

My husband was now willing to do anything to make it up to me. I asked him to come with me to an anniversary dinner of my parents' friends that evening. I wanted to show the world what my Father had done for me. My parents had been taunted a lot, accused of going through my difficulties because they had given up their faith. I wanted everyone to see what my parents had received instead. My husband went with me that day and we got more attention than the couple who was celebrating! The whole city knew about us and to see my husband and me, holding hands and greeting everyone with true joy radiating on our faces was a big shock. Everyone's eyes were on us. My shame was taken away and my Father placed a crown of honour on my head. I felt great and so did our parents.

Within a week, we were on our way back to Nigeria, where I met more shocked faces than happy ones. Anyway, months went by and I was constantly questioned by my family about our physical relationship. Everywhere I went, I was made to feel that nothing was perfect, that I had made a compromise. I had to show them that all was well and for that I had to have a child. I prayed every day. I had returned in January 1995, and it was already November.

I got stubborn with my Father, knowing that He could do it for me again. Many people told me that I could not insist on having something and because

God knows all things, He would not give me what was not good for me, that we would not give our children ice cream if they had a cough. Well, the Daddy I knew by now was the one who could take away the cough and give me the ice cream. So I continued to pray and became more specific about what I wanted: a daughter who would be born normally unlike my son who was born by c-section, a six pound baby unlike my son who weighed only two pounds. I was clear that I wanted to announce to the world that I was pregnant before Christmas and prove man wrong.

My Father did it again. He always does. Although my husband had not touched me yet, I started behaving as though I was pregnant. My sisters-in-law even commented on my behaviour and I acknowledged that I was pregnant not because I was, but because I knew my Father. When I was five months pregnant, we moved home and because I was big and could not do much, it was my husband who did all the moving. As superstitious and god- fearing as he was of his gods, he did not move them. He moved everything but left them behind in that room where they had once attacked me. My husband did not know my story but yet He was changing. My prayers were being answered.

My daughter arrived on time, a normal delivery weighing six pounds. Even the labour was short and not so painful. My husband loved her. Now as was the custom we got calls from India telling us what to name her based on the time she was born and the position of the stars at that time but my husband just announced that her name was Michelle, a name

I had liked even before she was conceived. He did not care about the stars anymore. Gradually, he stopped going to religious meetings. We still did not talk about the God I served but he had so many friends who were Christians, they did the talking for me.

Ten years later, in 2004, my husband finally confessed my Dad as his Dad, my Lord Jesus as his Lord and it has been a wonderful walk together. Together we have seen our Daddy come through for us. Even as I write now, my son is studying in the States and my daughter Michelle is with us. It has been over 15 years and my marriage is strong, and getting stronger even as we are growing in love and understanding for each other. With my Daddy around, I am always expecting to get to the next level of glory.

Love you Dad, very much.

An Accountant Counts the Cost

Deepak Idnani Accountant in the UK

I am one of a number of Sindhis around the world who have chosen to become a follower of Jesus Christ and I would like to tell you how this came about. I was born in Pune, India on 31st December 1965. My family immigrated to England in September 1966, when I was 9 months old. Even as a small child, I knew God existed. I believed the blowing of the wind through the trees and the movement of white fluffy clouds across the sky to be the actions of God. My late father was and my mother is a Hindu, but Christian neighbours took my younger brother and me to Sunday school when I was five and he was four.

When the Sunday School teacher first mentioned the name of Jesus, something stirred deep within my spirit and I felt drawn to this person. In addition to learning about the Bible and Christianity at Sunday school, my brother and I learnt about the Hindu gods at home. We participated in the various pujas and heard the Sat Narain Katha in Sindhi on every full moon. These two faiths had many morals and principles in common but also some significant differences, which often confused me. However, my heart was deepening in its love for Jesus and I spent a lot of time praying to Him and reading my Bible.

Eventually, in autumn 1975, when I was almost ten years old, I believed strongly that I had to renounce the worship of statue gods and commit my life to the one Eternal Living God and His Son who had died to pay the penalty for my sins. So, one Sunday night, I knelt by my bed and asked the Lord Jesus to forgive my sins and come into my life. From that moment, I knew that I was accepted by God and would go to be with Him forever when I died.

Understandably, I was concerned about how my parents would react and I decided not to tell them but to continue going to the Sunday School for as long as they would allow it. In 1980, when I was 14, my parents felt that I was getting too interested in Christianity and asked me to stop going to church (my brother had already stopped going as he had decided he did not want to become a Christian). I still did not have the courage to tell them that I was now following Jesus and I decided instead to respect their decision and stop going to church until I was an adult.

However, I hid my Bible under my bed and would read it in the middle of the night and at the weekends. I kept praying that I would have the courage to be honest with my parents about my faith. Finally, in February 1985, during my first year at university, I was baptised in the Holy Spirit and received the boldness to write a letter to my parents informing them that I was a Christian and explaining the reasons for my choice.

Their reply expressed shock and concern and a desire to discuss the matter fully during the Easter vacation. After a long discussion, in which my brother was also involved, they agreed to let me follow my faith and get baptised. In May 1985, I was baptised at a church near my university in Sheffield, North England but my parents did not wish to attend. After a period of time, my parents came to terms with my decision and were very happy for me to attend church and participate fully in Christian activities. In fact, they have attended church with me on a few occasions.

Over the years, I have found the Lord Jesus enabling me to overcome anger, jealousy, fear, pride and other such negative feelings. He has given me a deep love for God and all people and has brought an inner strength to my life. This strength was most notably demonstrated in 1998, when I was diagnosed as having a rare autoimmune disease called Pemphigus Vulgaris in which the body starts destroying its own skin by raising large blisters all over because it mistakenly sees the skin as a foreign body.

My condition was brought into remission by high doses of steroids and immunosuppressants and, I believe by the direct intervention of God in response to prayer. The drugs were quite debilitating and I had to be away from work for a long time, but I took comfort from the experiences of the man called Job in the Bible, whose body was also covered with painful sores. During this time I was also strengthened by the prayers, encouragement and love of my family, relatives and friends from all faiths. I sensed the Lord's presence very close to me and found that I could accept His will even though it was hard. I opened myself up to receive His joy and peace in fullness of measure. Over the next two years God brought an almost complete healing, so that I now have only rare and isolated skin lesions and have been able to work again normally since 2001. In February 2005, I lost my father and experienced the Lord's tenderness and comfort during the difficult time of grieving. I am thankful to the Lord Jesus for giving me eternal life and for being my closest friend who is always with me through good times and bad. I can talk to Him about anything and trust Him to guide me and provide for all my needs.

The End of My Search

Mary Schulz (nee Mahtani)
Pastor's Wife in Canada

I come from what one would consider a very religious Hindu family. It was normal for us to attend the monthly ritual of Sat Narayan as a family along with other rituals and ceremonies. This was done in order to appease the gods, in the hope that they would be pleased with us. However, the more I participated in these activities the more I felt the emptiness within me. I now understand what St. Augustine meant when he said, *"Every human being has a God-shaped vacuum that only God can fill..."* It was this emptiness that I was experiencing that led me to begin searching.

Let me give you a little background to help put you in the picture. My father came to Africa in 1937 and settled in what was then known as Northern Rhodesia. He was from the Sindh Province which is now part of Pakistan. His move was as a result of his being orphaned due to the upheaval that took place prior to the partition. He began a small grocery business which prospered to the extent that he felt that he was in a position to support a wife. So he travelled back to India where he married my mother in 1944 before returning to Africa. I was born not very long thereafter.

At that time, the apartheid system was in effect in Northern Rhodesia prior to independence in 1964 and schools were divided depending upon what you were classified as. There were schools for the whites and also schools for the blacks. However, there were no secondary schools for those who were considered as people of colour as we were a minority. So, I was sent to India for my high school education. My first year was at Sanawar near Simla. From there I was sent to Pune to an Anglican Convent School where I spent the next five years without coming home to visit my parents. My school holidays were either spent at school or my late grandmother's place. When I was with my grandmother I would go with her to the temple. But what really bothered me was the way the Hindus treated their fellow Hindus. The Jamadars were treated as sub-humans. Apparently this was the accepted norm in the Hindu religion. But this was something that I found hard to stomach or even tolerate, to the point that it angered me.

The time spent at school however, was more beneficial to me. It gave me an opportunity to do a lot of reading as I had much time on my hands. I read such books as The Big Fisherman, The Robe and inspirational books written by Nurse Edith Cavelle, and of course the Bible. Although I was not permitted to attend services I could not help but be drawn to this man Jesus who did not segregate or look down on those who were less privileged by the world's standard, but instead reached out to them. I just felt drawn to Him. At this point I determined that I would follow and do what was written the Bible as closely as I understood it. I began to align myself to the Word by changing certain habits in conformity with its teaching. A peace came over me that I had never before experienced. I then realized that I had found what I had been looking for - the Truth. This led me to write my parents requesting theirpermission to allow me to attend services. However, they did not even bother to respond to my request. I began to seek the Lord daily in my devotions and on my return to Zambia, I told my parents that I had converted to Christianity. Of course my understanding of being a Christian was going to church, reading the Bible and following Jesus.

I began attending services at the Anglican Church since it was in this denomination that I had been introduced to Christ. But my parents were not too pleased with my change of religion and forbade me from attending church. Rather than be disobedient to them, I stayed home and listened to messages on radio and watched ChristianTV instead to help me grow spiritually.

My life at home was not easy. The hardest part was when it came to the Sat Narayan Puja where I was compelled to sit with the family during these rituals while at the same time excusing myself from participating. (Here I am reminded of Naaman in the Bible) I did not want to offend the family while at the same time I wanted to please God rather than men, knowing that they did not know what they doing because they were in the dark. I had to love and respect them in spite of this; and prayed that the Lord would open their spiritual eyes and bring them to Himself.

In spite of all this, God was faithful in bringing people into my life who were instrumental in making me realize that one was not saved by just reading the Bible and going to church, but one had to be born again in order to be saved. It was only seven years later that I accepted the Lord Jesus Christ into my life as my personal Saviour while I was in London. In the book of John in the Bible we are told that, *"But as many as received Him, to them He gave the authority to become the children of God, even to them that believe in His name."*

It was then that I understood that I was now a Christian or a child of God as Jesus had now come into life to be a part of me and I a part of Him. It is only through confessing Jesus as Lord that one is saved. This salvation involves the cleansing or washing away of all our sins and making us righteous before the Father. Without this act we are separated from God and dead to Him, still living in the dark. At that point I was attending the church where Rev. John Stott was the minister. Though being Anglican, he had written several books on being born again. It was at this point that I had 'Moksha' and was united with Christ — the 'Jivan Mukti.'

This is the goal of all those who try to reach God through alms, fasting, rituals and ceremonies in the hope that they will attain this state. But no matter hard they try, it is impossible to do so. Our works are as filthy rags for only the blood of Jesus can cleanse us from all sin. And it is only through Him that we can live a life that both pleasing to God and victorious; for it is the power of God at work in us that makes us victorious and holy like He is.

On my return to Africa, I began to attend a Baptist Church where the pastor was a good Bible teacher and preached messages that were relevant and applicable to life, and not something abstract.

And since he was open to the things of the Spirit and demonstrated and encouraged the congregation to flow in the gifts of the Spirit, it became much easier for me tie what was being preached to that which was being done. It became real for me. Evidently these experiences really gave me a greater hunger for more of God and what He had in store for me. So, I left myself open to Him to use me in whatever way He chose to.

My Christian walk has not been that easy. In my desire to please God in what I did I was misunderstood by many who viewed things from a purely human perspective. My goodness and kindness was taken to mean that I was compromising myself and was accused of things that I was not doing. This hurt me very much. I have always wanted God's Word to have pre-eminence in my life at the exclusion of the traditions of men. And I will continue to base my choices on His Word and pray that it will always be so.

It was for this very reason that when the time came for me to get married, the scripture that came to mind was that found in Corinthians (2 Cor 6:14) which says, *"Be ye not unequally yoked with unbelievers."* At this point my parents had on two occasions found me somebody to marry as is the custom in the Sindhi traditions. But I did not want to be unequally yoked so I wrote them both stating my position and what I stood for. And that in order for me to marry any of them it was necessary that they become Christians so that we could have a common direction and source of strength. Needless to say, no betrothal took place. However, this did not stop my parents pursuing the issue of trying to marry me off. So, when I was 21, I was sent to India to attend my cousin's wedding with the hope that whilst there, they would link me up with someone and my aunt was given the task of finding a suitable husband for me.

I was in a dilemma. If I refused to go I would be disobeying my parents. And if I went, there was a chance I would be married to someone who was not a believer. So I went to India, praying to God to save me from a situation that would dishonour Him. By this time a man had been found who matched me and I supposedly matched him according to the priest. It had progressed to the point where my future mother-in-law had come to view me and approve since her son was resident in Singapore. She liked what she saw. But I did not like what was taking place. I fervently sought the Lord and asked Him to intervene.

God was faithful and came through for me. I was led to check my passport only to discover that it was about to expire. I went to the British Embassy where I was denied a renewal and told that I should obtain either an Indian or a Zambian passport since Zambia was now an independent country. I did not want an Indian passport as I considered myself to be Zambian since was born there. The problem was that the Zambian Embassy was in New Delhi and I was in Bombay.

I approached my aunt with the problem at which she gave me an option of either postponing the next meeting or forgetting the whole thing all together. I chose to forget it as he was not a Christian. "Praise

God!" He works in mysterious ways His wonders to perform. It was from here that I went to England where I was born again whilst in an Evangelical Hostel while I waited to enter university. During my last year I met a nice young Indian man who was pursuing a doctorate in civil engineering but he was a Jain by religion. Since he was interested in me, I made it clear to him that he had to be a disciple of Jesus if he wanted me to marry him. He assured me that he had been going to church but had not made a commitment.

I completed my university and returned back to Zambia where I waited for him to make a decision. Three years later he wrote telling me that he could not give his life to Christ as he had lost his father and felt that it would break his mother's heart if he were to change his religion. I took that to be a 'no.' Two months later I met a man who I realized was the man for me. But at this point he was a Roman Catholic — by name only as he had stopped going to church for a number of years. I however, made it clear to him that I did not want to be married to someone who did not believe as I did.

Since he had been disillusioned with church, I invited him to attend the church where I was now going. He readily came and as a result accepted the Lord a few months later. I had then to let my mother know of my decision (as my father had passed away a few years before this) that I had found someone whom I believed was the man for me. My mother was not pleased as he was not Sindhi but of mixed origin. To compound the issue he was not rich. Naturally, there were many factors at play here;

there was the issue of what the community would say, and whether I would be happy and whether the marriage would even last. Any mother would be concerned. I assured her that I believed the Lord was in it and He would see us through. That did not give her the assurance she needed and she could not release me with her blessing. As a result I had to wait nearly three years before she relented. Meanwhile I took the opportunity to explain to her that I was not interested in any dowry; all I wanted was her blessing and that of my brother whom had taken up the responsibility after our dad's death. Eventually they gave us their blessings and we married in March 1976.

After we were married my family accepted my husband and we now all have a wonderful relationship. God blessed us with a great home, which we dedicated to the Lord for His use, and three wonderful children. We both felt a call of God on lives. Then in 1986, my family released me from the business so that we could attend Bible school. We first went to Norway where we did a year of Bible school before proceeding to the States for another two years. On completion of the two years we went back to Zambia where we started church in another city from the one where we had started the first church prior to our going to Bible school. In the first city we were also involved in ministry. All the work still continues.

Then in 1997 we moved to Canada where we presently reside. We moved to a little village in 2004 where we again started another church and which my husband pastors. Yes we have come a long way;

but God is still working and drawing men unto Himself. It is definitely a privilege to be used of God in whatever capacity He chooses to use us. And it is encouraging to see people coming to salvation. There is no salvation in any other except through Christ; for it is in Christ that we are one with God — Samadhi.

My prayer for those who are still searching although somewhat in the wrong place is that they will come to the Way the Truth and the Life even as I did. My search is over. For I have found that which has filled the vacuum in my life. The same can be true for you dear reader.

Coming to Christ Through a Muslim

Dinesh Panjwani
Doctor in India

My name is Dinesh. I was born in 1972 to Hindu parents in a Sindhi household in the city of Mumbai. Being brought up in a Hindu family, we were taught that all gods were one, but our god was Guru Nanak. We would go to the Gurudwara only once a year on Guru Nanak Jayanti; other than that we hardly went to any temples for worship. I remember my mother keeping a fast every Thursday and praying to our god. There was a small mandir in my house to which I would go in times of need, for example, when taking an exam.

In junior college, my pluralistic view changed to an agnostic one. I had my friends, my parties, my play and not a care in the world, not even for God. Then it came time for me to go to medical school. It was there I met Hussain whom I had known for many years as a school mate. Hussain was a devout Muslim, but towards the end of the first year something unusual happened. I heard that he had become a Christian. I remember going to meet Hussain, who had always had a frown on his face, now smiling. He said these words to me, "Dinesh, the Allah that I used to worship was very hard on me and would punish me for all my wrongdoings; but the God (Jesus) that I worship now is a loving God and has mercy on me when I ask for forgiveness." Those words stayed in my mind.

Hussain would visit from time to time and share

the gospel with me. At one point I remember saying to him, *"Hussain, you can come to my house, but I am not interested in taking God and religion seriously at this point of my life, so please do not tell me about Him."* Hussain agreed but continued to pray for me.

A year later, I met the friend who had been instrumental in leading Hussain to Christ and we became good friends. He was a loving gentlemen and a man of principles. He would go out of his way to help me in my studies and occasionally told me about the saving grace of God. His life was very different from others that I had seen in all my life and I began to respect him. Together with Hussain, he would often invite me to Christian Bible studies but I never attended. Then, in September 1995, I decided to attend one time. I did not feel very different while in the study but was very happy to meet new friendly people. Having grown up in a Jesuit school, I did not feel it strange to be singing songs to Jesus. It was in that meeting that I was invited to go for a two-day Christian retreat, and I accepted the invitation.

There were twenty-four of us who attended the retreat. Most were meeting each other for the first time but I noticed that that every one of them was able to relate to each other in a friendly manner as though they had known each other for many years. This was very different from my previous experience. I felt it should not be that way and this bothered me. I felt there was something lacking within me, as though I did not have something that all these people shared and I could not understand what it was.

At the retreat, someone had just taught a

session on 'having quiet time with God' and had presented me with my first Bible. We were then asked to read a given passage from the New Testament and write down what we had learned from that passage. I tried and tried to understand that passage but just could not make head or tail of it. While others wrote sheets of paper on what they had learned, I had nothing. Feeling totally deficient, I went to Hussain and shared my feelings with him. He explained to me about my sinfulness, my need for a Saviour and Jesus as the only Saviour who washes away the sins of the world — if we believe.

So, I believed in my heart and Hussain prayed with me. Even at that time I was not sure what I was doing. Many thoughts were racing in my mind. What are my parents going to say about this? What does this mean? Will I have to give up all my 'normal' friends to follow Christ? Being confused, I went to another Christian friend and told him how I felt. He said, *"Dinesh, you need to count the cost of what it means to follow Christ."* At that point of time, I did not understand what he meant, but after many years, I now have realized the truth of my friend's statement.

After the retreat I started to read the Word of God diligently. I started with the epistles of John and just ate up what I was reading. For the first time, I felt as though God was speaking to me specifically through His Word, and my life started changing. My thoughts started changing. I felt a peace in my heart that I had never felt before. That was the beginning of my journey with Christ, which began on the 24th September 1995.

Then came the first trial of explaining my new

found faith to my parents. God has blessed me with two very understanding parents who, despite not knowing why I had begun following Jesus, trusted me and did not get in my way. The second more fiery trial was telling my girlfriend. We had been seeing each other for seven years at that point and were committed to be engaged and married in a year. When I told her I loved her but now I loved Jesus more than her, it came as a shock to her. I was hoping that she would one day become a Christian and we would be married as Christians. Soon I understood through the Bible that it was against God's Word to be married to an unbeliever. However, we went ahead and got engaged. In the Hindu context, an engagement is almost as big an affair as a wedding.

Soon after, I realized our ways of thinking were now going in totally different directions. My likes and dislikes had now changed. I wanted her to know Christ and on a number of occasions attempted to share the gospel with her but she would immediately become defensive and refuse to hear anymore. It became clear to me at that point that marrying an unbeliever would mean a life full compromise.

One day, a month after our engagement, I gathered the courage to tell her that I could not marry her and disobey the Lord, unless she became a Christian. Not surprisingly she was very upset. The next day I was summoned by her parents. I explained to them the reasons for not going ahead with the wedding. They were very angry and kicked me out of the house. Even though I loved her and wanted so much to marry her, I knew I had done the right thing in obeying the Lord.

Later that year my father became very ill and was rushed to the hospital where he had to be given cardio-pulmonary resuscitation and was revived. He was in the Intensive Care Unit and I prayed to God for my father's health. He quickly began the road to recovery. It was at that point I made my decision to serve God in missions. I wrote to Emmanuel Hospital Association (EHA) and was then sent to Herbertpur Christian Hospital at the foothills of the Himalayas. It was there I was baptized and met my first mentor who trained me surgically and also in evangelism. During that time I realized my call to be a career missionary in the villages of North India. I was in Herbertpur for three years and then went on to do my residency program in surgery at the Christian Medical College in Ludhiana, Punjab. After finishing my residency program I was posted again with EHA at Landour Community Hospital for a period of nine months. That was where I met Shannon, who would one day become my wife.

During the summer of 2003, Shannon and I were asked to go to Bihar as part of a team to one of the smallest hospitals within EHA. This hospital was on the verge of being shut down because of the lack of patients. We were given the time span of one year to see some change come about. Shannon and I were married May 2004 and resumed work at Madhipura Christian Hospital (MCH). We remained there until the fall of 2008 and by God's grace, we were able to see the hospital thrive once again.

My Journey from Karma to Grace

Administrator in Hong Kong

I was brought up in a rather staunch and conservative Sindhi family of six siblings with the understanding that there is a universal God and that all religions lead to the same God! Religious customs and beliefs were strictly observed in my family, which included observance of auspicious days and Hindu festivals. As obedient children, my siblings and I followed the customs and beliefs handed down by our parents. As the eldest daughter, I was also trained and groomed by my mom for my later married life which included the knowledge of how to take care of the home and skills like cooking and sewing. I was even taught how to perform religious duties (sewa) at the altar in our home, which included lighting incense sticks, chanting songs, bathing and dressing the various statues.

Hence, the concept of one God in many different forms, the awareness that we have to serve our karma because of past lives, among other beliefs, had been instilled in me ever since my childhood days. Yet, in spite of knowing and doing all that I was told to do, I still had no genuine peace or any assurance of spending eternal life with God after death. Instead, I felt miserable and spiritually empty. I always failed to do good "karma" as I had constant struggles with sins of jealously, lying, cursing and swearing. This went on until one day the Lord used my aunties to share the good news of

Jesus as they themselves had become Christians quite recently.

I did not welcome the good news right away. In spite of my own spiritual emptiness, I still argued with them about Jesus being the only way... until I noticed a big change in their lives. I was now curious and wanted to know more of their new so-called God, as I could not deny that it must only be the power of God alone who could have changed them. So, I began to read the Bible they gave me.

The scripture from Jeremiah 29:13 began to make sense. *"You will seek me and find me when you seek me with all your heart."* God knew that I was seeking Him and wanting to please Him by doing what is right, so He brought my aunties to open my spiritual eyes. I began to understand the things revealed through His word — the Bible, and His everlasting love and His forgiveness to me. What a relief to know the truth that there is only one life to live right here on this earth, and that I do not need to pay anything or anyone back for my bad karma from my previous lives. Instead, I was assured that from the moment I received Jesus into my heart and believed in Him as the Son of God, that all my past sins since childhood were completely forgiven! I could now start afresh, knowing that my past had been buried because of what He had done on the cross for me.

I thank God for His love that He sent my aunties to open my spiritual eyes. Not only did He give me the genuine peace I had longed for, but He also set me free from the sins I was struggling with and He continues to give me the power to live a less sinful life. At times, even when I do fall, I quickly turn back to Him as He is always there, ready to pick me up, to forgive, love and guide me again.

Soon after accepting the Lord, I stopped worshipping the statues. Initially, I was afraid they might harm me, especially at night - but the Lord assured me that He would protect me, and indeed He has until this very day. Soon all my brothers and sister accepted the Lord. My parents became very upset when we refused to pray to their gods or even join in any of the family's religious rituals. They felt hurt and rejected and thought that we were forsaking them and our culture. But thank the Lord that over the years, our lives have proven to them that having Jesus in our lives has made us love and care for them all the more. In August 2009, my dad accepted the Lord and obeyed Him in water baptism. We are now praying that my mom too would make the decision to follow Christ.

A few years after my salvation, my grandmother and my parents arranged my marriage to a man who was not a believer. I could have said no, but because of the fear of being disobedient to them, I gave in to their request. I finally pleased my parents but failed to stand on God's word.

After our marriage in India, everything seemed okay. My husband was very good to me and soon we left for HK where he had grown up. It was not long until I began to feel very lonely and lost spiritually, and almost thought I had left Jesus in Jakarta. I did not look for a church or associate with other believers. Instead I began to concentrate on other things...and soon left the Lord aside.

Then things began to go wrong! We lost our first son at birth, my husband lost all his money in the stock market, incurring huge debts and worst of all, my in-laws began to blame me for all this misfortune. Things became unbearable and for the first time after many months I cried to Jesus. God allowed all these things to get back my attention to Him. Slowly, I began to understand why He placed me in this situation and why His word clearly speaks against being unequally yoked. How can I live as a life-partner to a man whose ways are not of God's but of this world's? I was almost at the point of giving up on my marriage, and after much counselling I decided to live separately.

But thank God for His mercies and for hearing my prayers and those of my children, because finally after enduring for 19 years, I began to see the Lord's intervention! Within a period of 6 months of our separation, my husband lost both his father and his dearest sister in fatal illnesses - it was as though the Lord was speaking to him in many ways, until he too realized his need of a Saviour! This was the beginning of a turning point in his life and the Lord's turn to work on him! Soon after that we got back together and re-dedicated our marriage to the Lord in July 2000. Since then, our marriage (in spite of occasional ups and downs), has gradually soared upwards... to a point where I can say that right now, I am enjoying the golden days of my marriage life. Indeed, the Lord has good plans for our future!

Although I deserved to reap what I sowed in disobeying the Lord's word, His grace and mercy sustained me all along and I could see the Lord's loving hands teaching and moulding me day by day. In spite of having gone through obvious trials in my life, He has not allowed me more than I could bear (1 Corinthians 10:13). Indeed in my difficult times, he had proven to be my source of strength and hope with the support of my Christian family and friends. I can testify that Jesus has been true and real in my own life amidst all the struggles, and there is so much peace and joy as I put my future in His hands, while believing the promise in Jeremiah 29:11 that He has good plans for my future!

My genuine search led me to this one True and Living God. The joy and the peace I received are so much more than what the world can offer! He has been my comfort and my friend in this journey of life. Like a shepherd always there for his sheep, I am assured that He will never take His eyes of me. I have never regretted one moment since I asked Him to come into my life, and I have dedicated my life to serve Him as long as I live. All the wonderful promises in His word become mine...what more can I ask for!

Finding Jesus in Blue Jeans

Mohan Utamchand Vasandani
Businessman in Indonesia

My name is Mohan Utamchand Vasandani. I am Indian by birth and from the Sindhi ethnic group. My province, Sindh, is in Pakistan. Benazir Bhutto, ex-Prime Minister of Pakistan, also hails from Sindh, we both speak the same Sindhi language and write in the Arabic script. At the time the state of Pakistan was born, my family were the Hindu minority in the Sindh province which was predominantly Muslim. We had to flee from our homes in Sindh during the time of partition; there was much strife between Hindus and Muslims. I was born in May 1947, the partition happened in August, 1947 so I was only 3 months old at that time. We left Sindh and went to Mumbai and then by ship to Batavia (now Indonesia), where my grandfather and father had already developed a business (our family has been in Indonesia since 1895!)

My family were devout Hindus and at a young age I was introduced to the many gods that Hindus believe in. I was diligent and disciplined in performing all the Hindu rituals. I went to a Catholic school, Regina Pacis School, where many of my teachers were nuns and priests. After graduating from school I went to India for further studies at college and in 1966, returned back to Indonesia. During the early 70's, I became a devotee of Maharishi Mahesh Yogi, he became my Guru and I was taught Transcendental Meditation (TM).

On May 1,1977 I joined Levis Strauss Licensee in Jakarta, starting as a junior salesman and then working my way up to become the marketing manager. On April 18, 1982, I was in Ambon, a city located in the East of Indonesia for business reasons. Levis had a dealer in Ambon, who had a store called 'Mardika'. The owner's name was Sasanto. I met the owner and started to talk to him about business. At that time, Sasanto the store owner asked me about my faith, meaning my religion, and I told him I was a Hindu. He then told me that he was a Christian and tried to tell me about Christ.

I strongly protested and told him that Christianity was only about 2000 years old, while my Hindu religion was much older, how could he compare! Santoso then asked me for the name of my God. I was somewhat baffled and told him that Hindu Gods came in many names... Brahma, Vishnu, Shiva, Parvati, Ram and Ganesh are just a few. Santoso then told me to hurry back to Jakarta and find out the Name of the one true God. On April 19, from Ambon I flew to Makasar, the capital city of South Sulawesi. I reached Makasar at about 6 p.m. and by 6:30 p.m. I was at my hotel. I had a shower and then went down to the lobby to book a meeting room for the dealer's gathering that I was to have on the morrow, had my dinner and then at about 11 p.m., I headed back to my room.

As I entered the room, for no reason, I was gripped with fear. My wife called me from Jakarta, relayed to me news which was not good, which made me even more fearful and disturbed. I was angry with my wife for having called me only to relay bad news. I banged down the phone and went straight to bed covering my face with the white bed sheet. I then put my right hand on the right hand side of the bed and came across a thick maroon book lying on the side table; Holy Bible was written over it. I sat up in bed and started flipping over the pages, read the note about the Gideons who had placed the book, and went to the help section.

Under 'salvation' it said John 14:6. I flipped the pages to the verse referred and read, *" JESUS SAITH UNTO HIM, I AM THE WAY, THE TRUTH, AND THE LIFE: NO MAN COMETH UNTO THE FATHER, BUT BY ME."* After reading this passage, the fear that was in me was gone, there was utter peace that was beyond understanding. I slipped out of bed and sat on the floor beside the sill of the bed and was in tears realizing that Jesus was my Lord and Saviour! I was on the floor until about 5 a.m., then I had my shower and at about 7 a.m. went down to the lobby and called Brother Santoso in Ambon. I spoke to him for many minutes, not caring about the cost of the telephone call and repeatedly said to him, " BETA PUNYA TUHAN PUNYA NAMA YESUS, YESUS........YESUS!" (My God's Name is Jesus. ...Jesus.... Jesus !). That is how I came to know my precious God and Saviour.

I did not choose to be a Christian. How could a devout Sindhi turn to Christ? It is beyond belief... it was definitely Jesus who had chosen me, it was by His Grace that I was saved; the Holy Bible by the power of the Holy Spirit can bring any man to Jesus! I returned to Jakarta and for almost a week I did not tell my wife. I was sure that she would think I had gone crazy! I called my friend Ramesh who had turned to Christ a few years ago and told him what had happened to me. The first words that came out from Brother Ramesh were, "Praise the Lord, Praise the Lord." Brother Ramesh told me that he was a Gideon; it was people like him who placed God's Word in hotels. He took me to his church worship service, Assemblies of God, and within two weeks I became a member of the Gideons. Truly God's ways are not our ways!

All the members of my family have since come to Christ. When I came to know Christ we were only a handful of Sindhi Christians; today there are four Sindhi churches in Jakarta, and there are about four hundred Sindhi Christians now. Praise the Lord!

I do not practice TM anymore as I realized that there is no way or method to acquire God. We cannot apply strategy; it has to be God's Grace. Man probably can attain his 'high' using meditation, but please note man's high has nothing to do with attaining God. Man's high is not God's high.

A person like Gandhi or the prophet Muhammad, despite their religion and being good people, cannot make it to heaven because of sin. I can make it to heaven, not because I am good and do not have sin, but I am made whole because Jesus died for my sins! God knew from the very beginning that there was no way man could come back to Him. Sin was keeping man and God apart. That is why God sent His Son Jesus to die for the sins of man, how else could man return to God! John 3:16 reads,

"For God so loved the world, that he gave his only begotten Son, that whosoever believeth in him should not perish, but have everlasting life."

I thank the Gideons for their work. God Bless them. How could I have been saved, if that maroon coloured Holy Bible was not in that hotel room? We surely have a Miraculous God.

All Glory, Honour, Praise and Thanks to the Lord of Lords ...

Jesus is His Name ...

Jesus is His Name!!

Finding True Peace Aged 87
It's Never Too Late

Bhagwanti Pritamdas Chandiramani in Singapore

I am Mrs Bhagwanti Pritamdas Chandiramani, an 87-year old Sindhi widow. Since my husband's passing away in August 2001, I had felt very lonely and life seemed empty and meaningless. My health had not been good as I had been suffering from low blood pressure, then high blood pressure, with frequent headaches, dizzy spells and insomnia.

Medical check-ups were frequent and I was taking numerous types of medication. I would often tie a bandana around my head as a compress to help alleviate the persistent headaches. Furthermore, I had gradually lost mobility as my legs became very weak following a not totally successful hip replacement surgery. Also, issues with deep vein thrombosis, required my needing a wheelchair, which further limited my social activities and caused me to become home-bound and very miserable. I was often quite depressed.

In early December 2008, my health deteriorated further but I tried to keep it quiet. However, my daughter, who was then visiting from Indonesia, noticed how unwell I had become and alerted her brothers. Sensing the situation was serious, my son called an ambulance and I was immediately rushed to Changi General Hospital Accident & Emergency Department, where I had passed out. The attending doctor advised my family that I had suffered a severe lateral stroke, and that it could be fatal. The doctor said that if I recovered, I could suffer partial or even total paralysis.

My children felt devastated and helpless. Those of my children who had not gone on vacation, started to cancel their plans, while the others, who were overseas, were called to return home. They were all preparing for and expecting the worst outcome. In hospital I was warded into the High Dependency Unit, where I lay motionless for some days. There were tubes inserted all over my body.

I was denied any liquids and feeding was done by a nose tube direct into my stomach. I was devastated. During that time, I realized my mouth was dry and very parched, my throat felt burnt and I had developed mouth ulcers. I was miserable and would often bemoan, "I am well-known in the Sindhi community as 'The mother with 7 sons' (I was always so proud of that fact), but am now reduced to total helplessness, unable to even get a drop of water to drink!"

Meanwhile, one of my Christian sons, who was then in Dubai, had been praying that God would send someone to minister to me during my last hours. Elsewhere, one of my other sons, who was then in Kuala Lumpur on a business trip, was in tears. He pleaded with his Christian partner to intercede and pray for me.

I am discovering how truly wonderful and amazing is the power of prayer! Not only did my son's business partner pray for me, he made arrangements for some Sindhi Christian ladies to visit me in hospital. They came to visit daily and, even when I lay unconscious, would pray over me, laying hands for healing and restoration. They would also sing Sindhi gospel songs in my hospital room and read from the book of Psalms in the Bible.

During one of their visits, when my Christian son (who had returned from Dubai) was with me, the Sindhi ladies shared the Gospel Good News. I heard for the first time that Jesus Christ cared for me, and that He had come to restore my broken relationship with the Heavenly Father. I was told how His death on the cross paid for my sin and His wounds for my healing. I was asked if I would repent, seek His forgiveness and accept Jesus as my Lord and Saviour. I willingly and readily did. Both my Christian sons were overjoyed when I accepted the Lord Jesus, in hospital that day. They believed it to be the result of answered prayer.

As the days progressed, I began to recover, and was moved out of the High Dependency Unit and into the normal ward. All that talk of stroke, paralysis and loss of function was gone. Only the lung infection remained, which required more treatment. Yet, I struggled with my condition, hated the idea of being hospitalised and kept insisting on going home, where I could determine what I would eat or drink. I was being stubborn, taking things into my own hands instead of surrendering to God. I challenged God and even told my Christian daughter-in-law that if Jesus loved me, I would be well and discharged by Christmas. "I will put up a Christmas tree and together we will sing carols, "Ding, dong bell, pussy's in the well." Of course,

I had not realised then what a true carol really was. But, true enough, I was discharged on Christmas Eve, December 24th, 2008.

Alas, I forgot my God and came home to be my own boss! No Christmas tree, no thanksgiving, just pure indulgence. I continued to participate in the Senior Citizen's pagan festivities at Sindhu house and even drank lots of ice-cold drinks. All too soon, I had to be re-admitted to hospital with acute chest and lung infections. The tubes were back in me again. However, both my son and the Christian ladies continued to visit and talk to me about God while in hospital. One day, I separately told them that I had been hearing a Voice repeatedly saying, *"Yesu, pyar hai, Yesu pyar gaya,"* (which means "Jesus is love, and Jesus loves me"). I wondered if a CD was being played out loud by the hospital staff or even by one of the other patients beside me. But neither of them had heard anything like it. However, I continued to hear the Voice on a few more occasions.

I soon came to realise, that the Voice was God Himself who had spoken to me and thus started my beautiful faith journey with Jesus, my Lord and Savior. My heart was opened. By His grace and mercy, I was chosen and by His blood, I was saved! I began to experience an excitement and joy I'd never known. Incredibly, my physical condition improved markedly, so much so that I wanted to leap off my wheelchair and run! My desire to know more about Jesus grew.

Even after my discharge from hospital in mid January 2009, the Christian ladies continued their fellowship visits to my home. I would eagerly look forward to our weekly gathering. They brought gospel music and pamphlets to read. Then amazingly, one day, through a British Indian evangelist couple who came to visit, a Sindhi New Testament Bible was made available to me. No such Bible existed in Singapore ever before!

Indeed, ever since I got that Bible and started reading it, my faith has multiplied. I would read it daily, several times, often even ignoring sleep. In one year I have already read the New Testament many times over, almost 10 times. I thoroughly enjoy every moment of my reading as I feel God speaks to me through His word. I have grown in my faith. I have been attending Barker Road Methodist Church (BRMC) and its Glowing Years Ministry, which has been a great encouragement to me. Almost one year after I committed my life to Christ Jesus, I was baptised on 26 December 2009 at BRMC, with family and friends sharing in my joyous celebration.

Sadly, Aunty Bhagwanti passed away peacefully in 2010. Her greatest desire was to tell others of how God had changed her life through His love, to make her last days so joyful and peaceful. Her prayer was for all her family, friends and loved ones to come to know that love too.

My Life After Death

Businessman in Hong Kong

I became a Christian fourteen years ago, and it has been a truly challenging journey so far. It has been a time filled with amazing victories for me personally, for us as a family, but also a time of great loss and pain.

I was born in Hong Kong and grew up there as our family has been there since the late 40's - both sets of grandparents finding their way to Hong Kong in search of opportunity and fortune. Not yet a year old, I moved with my family to Africa where my father was to look after a part of our family business, and where my younger brother was born. We lived in Africa for five years before returning to Hong Kong.

At an early age my brother and I got involved with the 'wrong' crowd. Just barely teenagers with cigarettes in our fingers, we thought we could take on the world. As the years flew by, our weapons of choice also changed, from cigarettes to joints, to needles and before we knew it we were sucked into the seductive world of drugs. The drugs took over so quickly, from just partying to being enslaved by heroin. Scheming and stealing just to meet our daily fixes was what our lives revolved around; my brother and I were literally partners in crime. The fun turned to fear, and the pleasure soon showed us excruciating pain. Our worlds were falling apart, we needed a miracle, and Jesus sent angels with a promise of freedom.

On the streets of Wan Chai, we were met weekly by Christians on outreach to share the love of Jesus with us. Imagine two kids looking for a drug dealer, being met with past addicts talking to us about Jesus setting us free - it was mind boggling and simply too crazy to understand. I began to wonder which of us were really on drugs!

But sure enough they kept coming back and sharing with us what God had done in their lives. These were not strangers; some of them we knew from school, from buying drugs on the street, from 'doing' drugs together. Deep down we were jealous and desperate. We started attending their outreach meetings and receiving prayer. It was an eye opener; I had not realized how bad things really were. As a drug addict, you learn very well how to spin stories and events, fooling the world and, in the process, fooling yourself. I was not interested in their Jesus, but I knew they had something I wanted - FREEDOM. I was hungry for the promises their Jesus was offering.

Through their continuous commitment and love I decided to join their Christian rehab - a 14-day detox programme without medication, just prayer. I knew the pains of withdrawal, so going into rehab with these Christians and no medication had me freaked, but still I went. The 14 days were terrible; I was not open to being prayed for, nor was I willing to take part in their worship. On the 14th day I left and in hours was back on drugs.

The next few months I spiraled downward; I overdosed twice and developed septicemia from using unclean needles. After a short spell in hospital

I went back to the Christians for help. I was hurting everyone around me including myself. There was an opportunity for another Christian rehab in the Philippines. The commitment was for one year, but at that time I feltI had no other options, so I went. I was hanging on by a thread.

I have realized after all these years, that God just does not give up. I used to think that God comes when we are desperate, but the truth is that God is always there but we only go to Him when we are desperate. It was there in the Philippines that I met Jesus for the first time, after fighting for so long and after trying to reason Him in my mind as untrue.

We were in the middle of an electrical blackout due to a wild typhoon blowing, and that night, worship had been by candlelight. I had been in the Philippines just a few months, and the whole prayer and worship thing was still quite new and strange to me. I made a decision to ask God that if He was real, then He had to show me. I simply said, *"God if you are real, show me."* It was at that moment I experienced a loving and forgiving God.

All the awful things I had done over the previous ten years flashed before me, and in moments Jesus cleaned and washed them away. I was not quite sure of what was happening, or why all these tears were falling down my face but I knew that without a doubt I had just met God. I just knew the more I let go, the lighter I felt and the freer I was. I stayed on for another year after rehab, and saw how God used me to work in the lives of so many others. I started receiving healing in my life, for things that were part of my childhood, adolescence, and even as an adult.

I moved back to Hong Kong, and started a small trading company with some contacts my father had given me. I met an amazing woman who would end up being my wife but it was a highly stressful time. I no longer had 24-hour spiritual covering as I did in the Philippines, I was fighting to be faithful and ethical in a business that was losing money, and all the while making sure the wedding was going to be a Christian one. I was having a hard time, but again I knew that the God that had saved me did not give up, and neither was I going to.

It was not until our second year of marriage that the company started making money; I believe God was grooming me in those early years, teaching and guiding me to be a righteous steward for the things he was preparing for me. Our wedding had been a Christian one, witnessed by the greater Sindhi community of Hong Kong - something I know put a twinkle in God's eye.

Early in our marriage my wife became ill; she was employed by an international school with a medical plan that covered her medical expenses. After much prayer, we decided that she should quit her job as the stress from work was only making her condition worse. With this step, it meant we would have to take on the burden of her medical expenses. Many times the difficult things in our lives are there to teach us, and built us into people that God wants us to be. The illness has been difficult, but through those times we have reached out to Jesus and have never come back empty-handed.

I remember a time just after our first anniversary, where my wife was very sick, and was in hospital for weeks. After coming through the relapse, she developed deep vein thrombosis from being in bed so long. The hospital bills were piling up, and I was freaking out. I was praying desperately. I was in the office late one night, sending out product offers to people around the world. It was about 11:30 p.m. and I was ready to head home when the phone rang. The client calling me had received my fax, but he wanted 50,000 units on the condition that the merchandise would be shipped in a week. I told him to hold on, while I picked up the other phone, called the factory manager at home, and amazingly he had 50,040 pieces in stock in his warehouse. I closed the deal right there. Two days later the money was in my account, two days after that, the goods were shipped by air, and a week later the client placed two more orders. I paid the hospital bills, the office and home rent that were overdue, and still had a little left over!

The last few years have been a journey of healing specific parts of my life and opening up amazing things in front of me. One resounding theme has been my role as the leader of my family: the 'businessman' and bread winner, the husband and best friend, the father and guide - it is so overwhelming, it almost makes me want to me crawl into a little cave and hide. But I know I can do it with God's help and that I can do it well by God's grace. My heart is changing, although not as fast as I would like, but I guess just fast enough that it does not explode.

My faith in Christ has enabled me to walk up to higher heights that I never imagined I would reach. I know without any doubt that I would not be alive if Jesus had not died. I give all praise and glory to Him.

Witchdoctors, Potions or Jesus?

Sheela Sitaldas Mahbubani
Housewife in Indonesia

Jesus answered, "I am the way, the truth and the life. No one comes to the Father except through Me."

My name is Sheela. In 1987, I suddenly developed a sickness. I felt a tremendous pain all over my body like ten fingers being pressed on my back. I vomited all the time, sometimes even vomiting blood. My body rejected all food and water and I could not sleep at night. I went from one doctor to another, each one ran a number of blood and urine tests and x-rays were taken but no one could diagnose the problem.

My family tried their best to get me treated but to no avail. Someone suggested a visit to the witchdoctor. Since I had tried all kinds of options, I agreed to do as suggested. The witchdoctor gave me a concoction of water and flowers to drink and a charm to be kept under my pillow. I felt much better after drinking the concoction and slept fitfully with the charm under my pillow. I could now eat and drink without throwing up and my body stopped aching. However, the following day when I woke up, my condition worsened. I cried in pain and shouted for help.

We made a trip to another witchdoctor. Each witchdoctor uses different methods and techniques to cure people. He touched my back, extracting nails from it and then gave me a drink of water mixed with his saliva. After drinking the water, I began to feel well again. I could eat, drink and sleep well. My body did not feel any pain. However, the following morning I experienced the same excruciating pain. My condition deteriorated, but I did not give up.

I had found hope in the witchdoctors, so I visited a third witchdoctor. This time the witchdoctor rolled an egg over my back. After having done so, he cracked the egg open only to find a ball of hair instead of an egg yolk. He muttered some spells and gave me some water and I began to feel normal again. But the same scenes repeated. I kept visiting witchdoctors one after another until I had visited seven of them! None of the charms and spells worked long term. I cried day and night in agony, screaming for help but no one could do anything. My parents decided to have me treated in Singapore but all tests proved to be normal. There were no indications of any illness whatsoever.

One day my brother-in-law, who was not a believer in Jesus, was told by his Christian friend to invite people from the church to pray over me. Since we had tried all other options, we did as suggested. Surprisingly, I felt better, though not completely well. I was still struggling within myself and I decided to end my life by setting myself on fire. As I was making my final decision, I heard a gentle, loving and sweet voice say, *"My daughter, I love you so much, I will give you My peace and My joy. I will heal you and restore you."* I tried to ignore the voice, went into the kitchen and reached out for the can of gasoline and a matchbox. My hands were weak and I had difficulty lifting the can of gasoline. The sweet and gentle voice kept coming back. I began to feel annoyed at the persistence of the voice and shot back. *'Who are You?'* The voice replied, *"Go to church."* I answered, *'Yes!'* No sooner had I answered, than I felt the love and peace of Jesus surround me with joy and happiness.

At that time I was living with my sister Jeana who was a Hindu in Surabaya. I immediately asked her if she knew of any church there. She asked me why I wanted to know. I told her about the gentle, loving and sweet voice telling me to go to church. Jeana asked me to ignore the voice saying it was the voice of the Devil! However, I insisted on going to church, so we did. On the way, I felt a kind of excitement. I felt the love and peace of Jesus. In church, the pastor asked if any would like to come forward and accept the new life given by Jesus. I ran towards the front and could strongly feel the presence of God. That day I went home filled with the peace, love and joy of the Holy Spirit. That night the Lord visited me and asked me to be baptized by water. As I struggled to make a decision, I heard a voice saying, *"My daughter, take a step of faith. Be baptized by water and I will restore you. You will see a breakthrough in your life."*

The following day I visited the pastor and told him about the voice I had heard. The pastor was supportive and said that it was what the Lord wanted me to do. So I took the step of faith and was baptized by water and gave myself to Jesus. As I was submerged into the water, I saw Jesus standing behind me with outstretched arms. He touched my back. I felt like a heavy load had been lifted off my back. In an instant, I was completely restored and healed.

Three years of suffering had brought me brokenness, fear and sadness. Night and day I had cried out for help. At last I had found my Saviour, my Jehovah Rafa, my Healer, Jehovah Shalom, my Prince of Peace and Jehovah Nissi, my Prince of Victory. Jesus Christ is the Son of God who was crucified and died on the cross of Calvary for our salvation and for our sins.

Now I have given my life to Jesus to be used for His kingdom and glory. I am involved in the ministry for the homeless, handicapped and leprosy. I am also ministering to the little children as a Sunday School teacher.

Jesus gave me the best! I want to do my best for Him. He gave me a new life and it is my heart's desire to love Him with my whole heart just as He loves me.

From Gunda to Grace

Dinesh Motwani Teacher in India

I was born and bought up in a Hindu Sindhi family. My two sisters are older than me and my brother is fourteen years younger. My parents always had an aspiration that their children should obtain a good education and become pillars of society. Since we were from a small town, the only hurdle was that we had one English medium school within traveling distance which taught only up to the eighth grade. So, in order to fulfill our dreams, my sisters and I had to leave our small town. We went to Agra, the city famous for the Taj Mahal.

Since childhood, I was a boy who was quiet and always lost in a world of my own. When I was sent to Agra for higher education, I was very excited, but as time went by I realized it was very difficult or me to cope with the pace and nature of the city. While struggling with the new environment, new school and new friends I had to make many independent choices, and in that course of selection I chose some wrong friends.

I still remember the time while I was waiting for the results of a high school exam, my friends persuaded me to smoke a cigarette. I feel that was my first step on slippery ground which led me to the world I had never thought of entering. It so happened when I was given a cigarette to smoke that I liked it, not the taste but the sense that I felt grown up, even though I did not even know how to smoke a cigarette, but just the smoke coming out of my mouth was enough for me.

One of the friends who instigated me to smoke cigarettes had an older brother who came to know about us smoking. He not only threatened his brother but also tried to threaten me. I decided to deal with him because I was afraid of the reaction of my family and I did not want the news of my new habit to reach them. But this guy was really big, so it was virtually impossible for me to challenge him. I decided to ask another circle of friends that had really strong guys in it to help. These guys were not local, so they had to fight their own battles, but they always emerged strong and had given me assurance that if I ever had a problem, any time, I could rely on them.

This was the first time that I was threatening someone bigger than I was, and I had mixed feelings. Inside I was scared as I did not know what the end result would be, but outside I had to show myself strong and that I was successful. My friend's older brother opted to compromise and promised never to say or do anything to me.

This success gave me the sweet taste of power. After this issue I started flexing my muscles on any boy who came in my way and, as a result, all the boys of my age and slightly older started respecting me. I was enjoying this new found power but this led me further down the slippery slope. As I started walking on it I moved from one level to another until the time when the boys of the whole city knew me very well and my power extended to half of the city. There was no area where I had no friends. There was no government office where I had no links.

Slowly, slowly people started calling me 'BHAI', which literally means elder brother and in my new world meant someone who has power.

By this time, I was in college and had lost my desire to study and become a good man, but I still wanted to get a degree as I knew that when an educated person gets arrested, they get better treatment and accommodation in jail. It was then that my relationship with my family became strained. I did not like to go home but would prefer to stay in the battle field and solve issues in my own way. As I became stronger and had a network of more than 500 boys, I was approached by political parties to help them during election time. In return they promised to give me political protection. I knew no bounds. Money, power, sex, alcohol and more was all available to me. I became a law unto myself: many people would come and ask for my help wherever they had problems in the city, as by this time I was well known.

Let me share one secret with you: on the outside I was a hero for many, but inside I was always scared, as I knew I had lots of enemies and one day someone was going to kill me. So, though I was very powerful I would never go out anywhere alone after 8 p.m. I would never leave my residence unless I had a few boys around me.

In this dangerous game, one of my close aides decided to take revenge for the wrong I had done against him. This fight crossed the borders of the city and reached my home town where I was very weak and the enemy was very strong. The only solution left for me was that I should kill him and his brother and run away, but I knew that this game of shedding blood would not stop there as his allies were equally strong. The chances were that after my running away, they would kill my family.

This was the first shock for me, when I felt helpless. The second shock was that I realized that all my school time friends were well settled and I was considered a useless fellow by them. They did not want me to visit them or talk to them as they were afraid of being associated with me. I felt alone again and realized that this was not what I had planned as the initial goal of my life. I wanted to live as a respected man, not as a man who was feared by others.

According to Hindu mythology, I was taught that the soul is eternal and when someone dies the soul leaves one body and enters another. Looking back at the entirely different path that I had taken and also not wanting my parents to pay the price for the things I had done and would do in future, I decided to put an end to my life, thinking that I would experience birth again in some other family and would start my life afresh. Though I knew nothing about satanic influence, I could see my own dead body lying on the floor. I started having blackouts, my hands started shaking, and I would get angry at the drop of the hat. I did not know what had happened to me. I think I was not in my right mind.

By that time one of my sisters had come to know the Lord Jesus. She realized that I was depressed and was struggling with serious issues, that I was involved in wrong things and would not listen to any good teaching. She told me that she knew I had some problems and there was a man, the pastor of a church, who had direct contact with God. She told me if I would go and share my problems with him, he would pray and tell me the solution. I thought this man might be a kind of witchdoctor who would do something mysterious and let me know what to do.

With this thought in mind, on 1st January, 1995, I walked into the church. It was a Sunday. I saw the people inside the church dancing and singing to the Lord. They were different from me, full of joy, and here I was, sad and depressed, full of sin. That day some evangelists had come to the church and one young evangelist was preaching.

As I came out of the church, I could remember nothing except one line that was ringing inside me. Jesus died for sinners. I also realized that I was a sinner. I came home, closed the doors of my room and prayed this prayer: *"Jesus, today I heard you died for sinners, and I am a sinner who is going to put an end to his life. If you can save me, then save me."* Beyond my imagination, Lo! He walked into my room and was standing right in front me. His appearance is beyond explanation. No amount of words will explain His beauty. He spoke with a deep voice, *"My son, I have given my life for you and you don't have to die in your sin."* I fell prostrate before Him and surrendered my life to Him, saying, *"From today onwards, I will live for you."*

From that day onwards He has directed my path. Meeting the Lord is a daily experience, not a one-time occurrence! Today my life has changed tremendously. I can say I am abundantly blessed.

I live a happy life with my family, the husband of one beautiful wife and father of three cute little angels. I am serving the Lord with my whole heart and will continue to do the same until my last breath.

My life did not end; my new life just started with the Almighty Living Lord Jesus to whom I give all my praises. AMEN!

It Took a Cessna to Crash for Me to Find God

Joti Dulamal Kapahi
Nurse in Philippines

October 16, 1990 is a day that shall forever be etched in my heart. It was a tragic day that began the spiritual journey of my life.

My name is Joti Dulamal Kapahi. Growing up in Dumaguete, a province in the Philippines, our family was everything to us seven siblings. We had the happiest time ever despite the lack of technology. Both my parents were Hindus and we studied at a Protestant school so we had a conflict of religion there. My father was determined to get us as highly educated as he possibly could so I have a sister who is a psychologist, my two brothers are doctors, I am a nurse and my other sisters finished mass communication and business courses.

I got married into a wonderful Hindu family in Manila in 1982. Life was so good I did not even need God in my life. My brother Rajan was the first Christian in the family. He was a practicing cosmetic surgeon who did charity hare-lip surgeries for the local people. My sister Asha was brought to the Christian faith by Rajan as well. She would call me very often to tell me about the Lord Jesus Christ but I would turn each conversation into a joke and tell her, *"When I die I'll just tell God I'm Asha's sister and I'll get into heaven on the grounds of affinity."* This went on for so long that I began to dread getting phone calls from her, knowing what was coming. Yet, she never gave up on her siblings and would continually pray for us despite our taunting her.

On October 16, 1990, the day before Diwali, my brother Rajan was called into an emergency. The 6-year old niece of a fellow Rotarian had been involved in a car accident and was thrown out of the vehicle suffering a head injury. Our local hospital was not equipped for neurological cases, so the child had to be transported to a near-by island. Commercial flights only flew once a day so my brother had to request a friend who owned a Cessna plane to fly them down to the island. Prior to leaving he called my mom to inform her that he was leaving for Cebu and would be back later that night.

He promised her he would be home for the Diwali puja to be held the next night. Upon reaching Cebu, the island he needed to bring the child to, he checked the little girl into the hospital, got her settled in and endorsed her to the neurologist. They were asked to spend the night but since my brother was on a 24-hour call, he opted to leave to return back home. They were in the vicinity of the Dumaguete airport when the tower radioed them to turn back as there was zero visibility at the runway. Turning back, they flew directly into the eye of a storm that lasted just 20 minutes and which caused the plane to crash into the middle of the ocean.

I got a call from home at about 5:30 in the evening of the same day informing me that my brother's plane had disappeared from the radar screen and that they were fearing the worst. That was the first time in my life I got down on my knees and prayed to a God I never thought I would believe in. I begged and cried for God to bring my brother back promising all sorts of things in exchange for my brother's life. But the continuous frantic calls from home gave me the nagging feeling that I had lost my brother. My family back home was told that if the plane had indeed crashed, it would have fallen into a shark infested ocean and that the strong sea current would have swept them into the South China Sea so it would be as close as impossible to retrieve any bodies. My sister's prayer group immediately gathered at my parent's home and started praying. My sister simply asked God to give her a passage of assurance from the Bible and she was led to Isaiah 43 which says, *"Fear not for I have redeemed you; I have summoned you by name, you are mine. When you pass through the waters, I will be with you; and when you pass through the rivers, they will not sweep over you. When you walk through the fire, you will not be burned; the flames will not set you ablaze. For I am the Lord your God..."* It was then that my sister knew Rajan was with the Lord. My parents got a call at about 4:30 the next morning informing them that my brother's body had floated to the seashore near home. That was the first miracle of God.

I flew home on the first flight the next morning and entered a house of mourning, a house that was normally a house of laughter. I collapsed at the sight of my brother's coffin. It was just surreal. Rajan was the life of the house, the most loveable person ever! This could not be happening to us! It was then I saw how broken my parents were. But, on the other hand, my sister despite her tears and pain was singing praise songs and glorifying her God.

I thought my sister had gone berserk! What was she doing praising God at a time like this! Then again, she was the solid rock for all of us siblings who were lost and angry with God. Yet, this was the first time I seriously listened to her talk to me about God's promises to her. I thought I would give her God a test and see if He was really a God I wanted to have in my life. I made a bargain with God, *"If you truly loved my brother, you will give me a sign that he is with you in heaven. If you do that, I promise I will accept you as my God too. I want you to send me a white feather as a sign of Rajan being with You."* Ha! Let us see how He sends a feather into a closed house.

Early the next morning, after a fitful night's rest, I was making my way to the living room where my brother's casket lay when, lo and behold, a white feather fell at my feet! No! This was a joke I thought. This could not be true! Did I ask God for something that was too easy? Maybe I should have asked for something harder than this. I called my sister's attention to it and she was ecstatic. *"Jo, God has answered your prayer!!"* Yeah, right. Now I had to keep my promise? As cynical as I was, I knew I had to keep my promise. I was afraid God would expel my brother from heaven and that would be on my conscience. As soon as I got back to Manila I went to attend a Christian service at a church my sister's pastor recommended. I tried it for a couple of months but did not feel I belonged there. A friend of mine told sisters Leah and Zinnia about my case and they

came to the house one day and invited me to the Fil-Indian Fellowship. To date this is my church and my extended family.

I am so grateful that the Hindu family I married into supported me in my search for spiritual growth and allowed me to worship my own God without condemning me. My fervent prayer now is for my own husband and children to accept Jesus Christ as their Lord and Saviour too. God has never let me down and I know, in my heart, He will claim them as His own too...one day very soon.

A Curious Mind Seeks Answers

Celia Mahtani
Teacher in the UK

I have an English name, but my parents were both from the Sindh province in India. They left India after partition, and went to England where they started a family. I am the second child, with an older sister, and while my mother was expecting me, she was hoping for a son. Everyone else in her family had had a son by the second child, so she prayed for a son and assumed that her prayers would be answered.

I grew up knowing that there was something wrong with me and that I was a disappointment, but I did not know why. It was never discussed but I just knew it deep within. As a result, I was a very quiet, withdrawn and shy child, but with a strong temper and sharp tongue.

We grew up as Hindus and did the rituals and pujas, but even though I helped my mother take care of the gods, clean the house and make prasad, I was full of questions. Why were we vegetarian on Monday? Was there a 'Karma scale' to know how we were doing? How could I stop my mind wandering during the puja? These are just samples of my questions. My mother arranged Hinduism classes for me, but my questions exasperated the teacher, and his answers did not satisfy my curious mind.

During a trip to India after I had finished university, my mother arranged a meeting with Dada

Jashan. I asked the same questions and the gist of his reply was that I needed to try harder. Of course he did not say this so bluntly, but that was the message. During the meeting I could not stop myself noticing his eyes. I felt there was no warmth in them; to me they were cold and hard. I also felt that I was trying as hard as I could to understand, and as a scientist I had been taught to seek answers, not just blindly accept what I was told. So I came away still dissatisfied, and my poor mother was also frustrated. If Dada Jashan could not answer my questions who could?

Later, in my twenties I wanted to get married to a man I had met. There was a major problem though: his family were from a different religion. Although my family were initially against the marriage, they reluctantly came to the place of being able to support our marriage, but his family were totally against it and refused to change their views. The crunch came on our wedding day and he had to choose: me or his family. He chose his family. I felt rejected and felt that he had broken all the promises we had made to each other, to be there for each other, come what may. My family also had the trauma of cancelling the reception, phoning all the guests, disposing of the food which went to a nearby nurses' hostel and arranging for the honeymoon tickets to be auctioned on a London radio station!

To make matters worse, I now had nowhere to live because I had given up my flat as I was getting married. My family were all abroad and the family home was rented out. I had also changed my name on my passport as we were going on honeymoon. My best friend was married to his best friend, so now they as a couple would have to choose between us, and, to cap it all, I was already using my married name at work, as it was a new job and my supervisor had suggested this would be easier for my clients. Now I was going to have to change my name and explain it was because I did not get married. I could not face all this, so I handed in my resignation, and the two weeks I had taken off for our honeymoon covered the notice period. I found myself jobless, homeless, friendless and hopeless.

I then became the subject of an urgent family discussion. What were they going to do with me? The family felt that I could not stay alone in London and eventually it was agreed that I would go and stay with my sister and her family. My parents were reluctant because they knew that she and her husband were Christians, but it was the best solution as their children were quite young, and everyone felt that the children would be therapeutic. There was also the practical side, she had the space and could do with the company and the help, and I needed people around me.

I packed up my things, knowing that for the short term I had people who were willing to care for me but without any idea about the future. My sister was given two instructions from my mother, *"Don't leave her alone,"* and, *"Don't convert her to Christianity."* To these two instructions, my sister replied, *"I cannot convert her, only God can do that,"* and, *"If I cannot leave her alone that means she will have to come to church with us on Sundays."*

My mother felt she could not disagree as there was no other option, although she was not happy. I soon settled into a routine of physical activity and busyness, helping with the children and household chores, but my mind was not settled, and my emotions were still numb - I did not feel anything, no pain, no anger, no joy, nothing. I knew that there must be more to life, but I did not know how to find it or who I could trust.

My sister encouraged me to go out and meet new people, so I started attending a group called the Young Adults Group (YAGS), which was mostly young singles from the church. One thing that really impressed me was that the Christians all seemed to be genuinely nice and friendly people. I expected them to be asking lots of questions and talking about me and my broken engagement, but that did not happen. Those that knew accepted that I was hurting, but I did not feel judged or that they regarded me as a bad person. They waited for me to be ready to tell my story and when I did, they appeared to be genuinely shocked, so if they did know already, they were very good actors!

My sister and her husband had a Bible Study group that met at their home before church on a Sunday morning, and again I had to join in, although very reluctantly. A few weeks after I arrived, the group had a weekend in the mountains, but I did not want to go. The same discussion came up; they could not leave me at home as they had promised my parents, so I had no choice. I agreed, planning to spend the days with the children, but as their childminders also came for the weekend, this plan did not work and I had to join the adults and the studies.

When we got home on Sunday evening, I received a phone call from my ex-fiancé in London. He had obtained the phone number from my best friend and had tried calling over the weekend while we were away. He said he was worried about me, and wanted me to go back to London. However, he could not give me the reassurance that I needed, that he would marry me in spite of his family. He told me to trust him that it would be okay and things would work out but I was still hurting very much and needed more than just words to convince me. I think I was hoping he would come out to me, but he did not suggest it, and I wanted it to come from him. I came off the phone feeling very confused wanting to believe him and trust him, yet not being able to.

I went back to the living room and my brother-in-law asked about the phone call. He had heard my side of the conversation, and had guessed what was going on. I told him I felt confused, I did not know who I could trust as this man who said he loved me had let me down so badly. My brother-in-law told me that actually there is no one on earth who would never let me down, as no person can guarantee to always keep his word. The only one who can guarantee to never break his word is God himself, as is written in the Word of God:

"God is not man, one given to lies, and not a son of man changing his mind. Does he speak and not do what he says? Does he promise and not come through?"

My brother-in-law asked me if I was willing to

trust this God, and His son, Jesus who died for me. All I could think about was that I could not trust people; this I knew only too well. Could I trust God? I was not sure, but what did I have to lose? If God let me down, would I be any worse off than I was already?

I decided that I was willing to try and trust God, as my situation could not be any worse than it was. My brother-in-law said a simple prayer and asked me to repeat the words he said. As I said those words, it felt like a huge load was being lifted off my shoulders, and for the first time in many weeks I felt free. My sister came into the room a few minutes later, having put the children to bed and her first words were, "You're smiling." She hadn't seen me smile since that fateful day when I was supposed to get married, five weeks earlier.

This happened over 25 years ago and I can honestly say that what my brother-in-law told me was true. God has never let me down, broken His word or changed His mind, and YES, I can trust Him. My mother was not happy when I told her that I was now following Jesus, but when she saw how I changed, becoming more patient and more at peace within myself, she realised that it was good for me. Her greatest concern then became to find a husband for me. Mothers never stop worrying, do they? But God solved that problem too, although it took about two years.

During that time I had to learn to laugh again and to trust people. Through the church I met many people who were around for just a short time as Geneva, where I was staying, was like a crossroads, with many people passing through. Each one helped me in the healing process in one way or another until I was ready for marriage. Through that group I also got to know a Sindhi man who is now my wonderful husband. I have two amazing sons who are more that I could have wished for or dreamed of and who also follow Jesus. My mother's dream was for both her daughters to marry Sindhi men, and this is what has happened, in spite of the scandal that I caused the community. Maybe marriages are made in heaven, after all.

Since I accepted Jesus, He has been teaching me to let go of all that I am holding on to and to trust Him in everything. Imagine being offered a new gift, but your hands are full of the old things you have. There is no place for the new until we can let go of what we are holding on to. When my eldest son, Arun, was two years old, he fell down and broke his front tooth. I was right beside him, but could not catch him in time, and we spent the afternoon at the hospital having x-rays and other tests. Through this experience the Lord showed me that as much as I love my children, I cannot protect them even when I am with them. He helped me understand that I have to entrust them to Him, and He will be there for them, caring for them and protecting them. However, I am a slow learner, as my younger son, Sanjay, also had a accident at a very young age, and God had to gently remind me of the same lesson again! He is so patient with us, no matter how slow we are.

More recently, God has shown me where my insecurities came from. One day, while I was praying, in my mind I felt like I was watching a film. I saw a baby lying in a crib, and a woman was standing next to the crib, shaking her head saying, *"It's another girl."* I knew the baby was me, but had no idea who the woman was although I knew it was not my mother. I burst into tears, and through my tears saw Jesus pick the baby up and say, *"She's precious to me, I will always look after her."*

The Bible reminds us that we each are unique, and that God loves us as we are. He knew us before we were born, does not make mistakes and has awonderful plan for each of our lives, if we are willing to seek Him and obey Him when we find Him.

This picture has stayed with me, and whenever I find myself feeling insecure or unworthy, I remind myself that I am precious to God, and that He loves me just as I am because He made me. God knows and loves each one of us, and the more we understand this, the better we can cope with all that life throws at us. People may try to control or manipulate us for their convenience, but God wants us to have His very best. He is calling you and me, but we have to respond to the call. When difficult circumstances arise we have a choice, to run to God or to run away from Him and try and find a solution on our own. I have realised that the best way is to turn to God. After all, He created everything, so He must be able to solve whatever is happening to me and therefore to you as well.

A Father's Love Letter

A Father's Love Letter is a compilation of verses from the Bible that are presented in the form of a love letter from God to you.

My Child,
You may not know me, but I know everything about you
I know when you sit down and when you rise up
I am familiar with all your ways
Even the very hairs on your head are numbered
For you were made in my image
In me you live and move and have your being
For you are my offspring I knew you even before you were conceived
I chose you when I planned creation
You were not a mistake, for all your days are written in my book
I determined the exact time of your birth and where you would live
You are fearfully and wonderfully made
I knit you together in your mother's womb
And brought you forth on the day you were born
I have been misrepresented by those who don't know me
I am not distant and angry, but am the complete expression of love
And it is my desire to lavish my love on you
Simply because you are my child and I am your father
I offer you more than your earthly father ever could

For I am the perfect Father
Every good gift that you receive comes from my hand
For I am your provider and I meet all your needs
My plan for your future has always been filled with hope
Because I love you with an everlasting love
My thoughts toward you are countless as the sand on the seashore
And I rejoice over you with singing
I will never stop doing good to you
For you are my treasured possession
I desire to establish you with all my heart and all my soul
And I want to show you great and marvellous things
If you seek me with all your heart, you will find me
Delight in me and I will give you the desires of your heart
For it is I who gave you those desires
I am able to do more for you than you could possibly imagine
For I am your greatest encourager
I am also the Father who comforts you in all your troubles
When you are broken-hearted, I am close to you
As a shepherd carries a lamb, I have carried you close to my heart
One day I will wipe away every tear from your eyes
And I'll take away all the pain you have suffered on this earth

I am your Father, and I love you even as I love my son, Jesus
For in Jesus, my love for you is revealed
He is the exact representation of my being
He came to demonstrate that I am for you, not against you
And to tell you that I am not counting your sins
Jesus died so that you and I could be reconciled
His death was the ultimate expression of my love for you
I gave up everything I loved that I might gain your love
If you receive the gift of my son Jesus, you receive me
And nothing will ever separate you from my love again
Come home and I'll throw the biggest party heaven has ever seen
I have always been Father, and will always be Father
My question is ~ Will you be my child?
I am waiting for you.

Love,

Your Dad,
Almighty God

Next Step on Your Journey...

Our desire in compiling this book has been to share our good news with you. We trust you have been encouraged and enriched as you have read the stories.

If you have been touched or inspired in any way by what you have read, or would like to get in touch with any of the people in this book, we would love to hear from you.

This is a very limited compilation of some 20 Sindhis who have come to faith in Jesus. We know of many thousands of others and we can assure you that there is a Sindhi follower of Jesus near where you are.

For the sake of the privacy and protection of those who have written their life stories, the authors reserve the right to screen all requests.

We invite you to send your comments, feedback and encouragement to:

SindhiJourneysofFaith@gmail.com

We appreciate your willingness to read this book and pray that God may continue to lead you on your own spiritual journey.